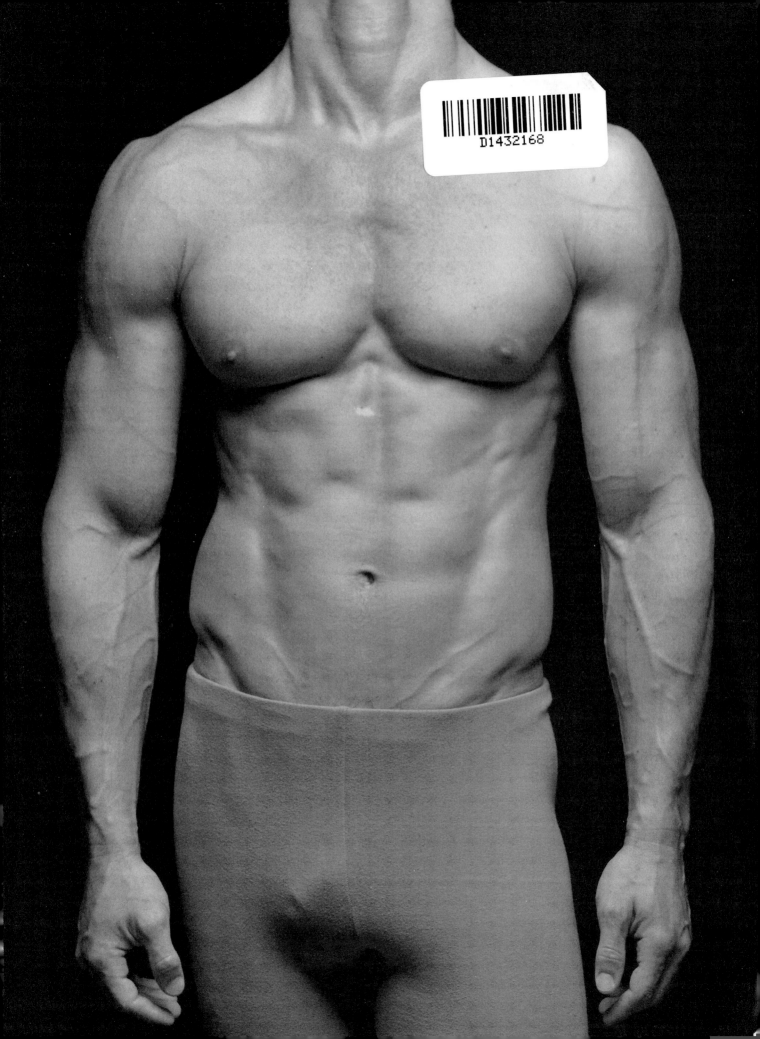

BASIC TRAINING

A Fundamental Guide
to Fitness for Men

JON GISWOLD

with photographs by
DAVID MORGAN

project direction by
KEN ROBERTS

ST. MARTIN'S PRESS ❈ NEW YORK

A NOTE TO READERS

This book is for informational purposes only. Readers are advised to consult a doctor before beginning any exercise program.

BASIC TRAINING: A FUNDAMENTAL GUIDE TO FITNESS FOR MEN. *Text copyright © 1998 by Jon Giswold and photographs copyright © 1998 by David Morgan. All rights reserved. Printed in the United States of America. No part of this book may be used or reproduced in any manner whatsoever without written permission except in the case of brief quotations embodied in critical articles or reviews. For information, address St. Martin's Press, 175 Fifth Avenue, New York, N.Y. 10010.*

BOOK DESIGN AND COMPOSITION BY GRETCHEN ACHILLES

Library of Congress Cataloging-in-Publication Data

Giswold, Jon.

    Basic training : a fundamental guide to fitness for men /
Jon Giswold ; with photographs by David Morgan.

    p.   cm.

    ISBN 0-312-19235-5

    1. Exercise for men. 2. Physical fitness for men. I. Title.

GV482.5.G57   1998

613.7'0449—dc21   98-21132

                                CIP

First Edition: December 1998

10 9 8 7 6 5 4 3 2

Acknowledgments

The combination of visionary people, together with the intensive creative process of putting a book like *Basic Training* together, was truly a satisfying collaboration for us all. Putting the pieces together seemed effortless once our team was assembled. For all of us, conveying this message to Michael Denneny was simple. He shared our enthusiasm and understood our vision, and was brave enough to do something about it. We thank him and his entire staff of supporters at St. Martin's Press: Sarah Rutigliano, Gretchen Achilles (design), and John Karle (publicity). We are honored to be part of your literary family.

To the professional men and women who encouraged this work and lent their time, expertise, and resources to create this book, thank you. Dr. Steven Victor, Dr. Richard Bachrach, Dr. Glen Weiss, Mary Ann DeLucy, Stephanie Donnelly, Gail Fisher (production manager and first assistant, Los Angeles), Joey DiGiandomenico (second assistant, Los Angeles), David C. Mendoza (groomer, Los Angeles), Jorgé Vargas (groomer, New York), Tom Shannon, Liz Grenier, Tom Kurthy, Stan Fednick, Kevin Roche, Eddy Trotter, Edward Bergman, Bobbe Vagel, Todd Huth, Steven Weissman, Walter Krause, Jeffrey Scott, David Lengen, Petra Kolber, Nicole Smith, Daniel and Estrellita Brodsky, Kieth Dodge, Enid Stubin, Susanne Freidrich, Renate Klein, George and Mary Pogacich, Chuck Adams, Martin Giswold, Roxanne Knops, Monica Buck, and Paul Meyer. Special thanks go to Marc Raboy and to Ken Miller for their perseverance and unlimited encouragement and to Houjing Lee for his artful talent and care for our images.

Locations and equipment were graciously donated for our unlimited use. We would like to acknowledge those who allowed us to use their homes, clubs, clothing, and equipment: Buzz Hood for the use of his house in Los Angeles, Jonathan P., also in Los Angeles, for his great house, Ashby and Pat Grantham for their house in Sagapanack, New York, the Montauk Oasis at Ditch Plains Beach in Montauk, New York, Anthony Ingrao for his Stone House in Montauk, New York, Paul Page, CRUNCH L.A., Roger Harvey, Columbus Place Fitness, Reebok Sports Club/NY, David Barton Gym, the Step Company and the Don Oliver Barbells, the Gym Source and Thomas Jackowski for his equipment, DKNY, Crunch Gear, Raymond Dragon Menswear, and Verge Menswear.

To the modeling agencies for their cooperation and for their handsome men. In New York—Zoli, with special thanks to Roseanne Vecchione. To Aqua, with thanks to Nigel. The Lyons Group, with special thanks to Mike Lyons. R&L and Wally Rogers for his help. And finally to Vehe and the staff at L.A. Models, thank you. This list of men isn't as impressive as the men themselves. Each brought his own energy to this project and we hope to make them all proud of their support: John Nies, Thom Fleming, Michael Harder, Jeremy Frisbee, Eric Feindel, Eric Von Frohlich, Bob Harper, Michael Anthony, John Mulling, Kevin Kiely, David Matthew Givens, Marcus Pourteau, Jonathan Prandi, David Carter, Dylan Michaels, Brett Birrittella, Darren Gough (front cover), Tony Antolino, Billy Zerillo, Herb Heffner, Lawrence Bullock, Neil Landy, Dalvane, Jim Brace, Kaleo Griffith, Vahé Shaghzo, Reeves Watson, Tim Elliot, Will Howe, Ivan Ortiz, Timothy Dipri, Dillon Silver, Lytel Young, Jason Maltas, David Honorel, Jason Sullivan, David Hay, Edon, Darin Lannaghan, Tom Torman, Timothy Thompson, Craig Demeter, Randy Henson, Chris Meagher, Andrew McOrmond (back cover), Meade Dickerson, Rod Schimko, James Stephan, Dennis Dassow, Noah Brody, Carlos Pertuz, Fred Harris, Mark Bohuslav, Charles Tripodi, and Tom Saunders.

Contents

PART ONE

Motivation

CHAPTER ONE

Introduction

WHAT BASIC TRAINING CAN DO FOR YOU

In these pages you will find exercises, activities, and photographs of men of all shapes and sizes that, I hope, will inspire you to begin a fitness program of your own. The most difficult part of embarking on such a program is finding direction: knowing where to start and at what level of intensity and how many times a week to work out. *Basic Training* is intended to give you that direction: to teach the exercises by guiding you through each move with perfect form; to create a personalized training routine that meets your needs and fits your schedule; to set realistic goals that you can accomplish while looking ahead to new ones.

When you say "I'm working out," I want you to refer not just to one day's exercise and weight-training regime at the gym or at home, but to a change in lifestyle that brings with it improved health and stamina, greater strength and agility, and a heightened sense of the possibilities and pleasures of life itself. The idea behind *Basic Training* is to present fit-

ness not just as a physical skill but as a positive, healthful, enjoyable part of your life.

In a way, beginning a fitness program is like learning a new language: You have to admit to a beginner's awkwardness as you memorize vocabulary words; you may stumble through your first simple sentences, but eventually you will develop fluency and the delight of expressing yourself in a new yet somehow familiar mode. Gradually, imperceptibly, you find yourself at home in this new world, and you don't ever have to lose this ability. *That's what having fitness in your life is about.*

A fitness program doesn't have to be a solitary, lonely business. This book may encourage you to meet others in a health club, at the beach, while sailing or playing volleyball, or at a city playground or park for some one-on-one basketball. The burgeoning of expensive, massive health complexes and sports clubs may create the impression that fitness is an elitist activity, but by its very nature,

fitness is inclusive, democratic, pluralistic—a lifestyle for everyone.

Throughout *Basic Training* I'd like you to consider your goals—improved health; a stronger, more flexible, more skilled body; an active and pleasurable lifestyle—not just as a *product,* the tangible result, of all your hard work, dedication, and commitment, but also as a *process,* the experience of the moment. The way I see it, getting there isn't half the fun; it's fun all the time you're doing it! Think I'm exaggerating? Consider this: How many of us stop in the middle of some wonderful experience to recognize our own pleasure in being? Exercise can provide countless examples of that kind of pleasure, the almost subconscious joy in living that can help us make it through tough times, invigorate our daily, mundane routines, and inspire moments of real transcendence, when we look past the ordinary, the familiar, into the realm of human delight. Call it spiritual recognition or call it an endorphin high, it's something to reach for and achieve again and again: *Be in the moment.*

"THE SECRET"

Many people believe there must be a secret to obtaining the "body beautiful." The truth is there are no secrets. You can change the way you look and feel by exercising, eating well, and focusing on the progress these changes are making in your life. But there are myths surrounding fitness, and I'm going to dispel them for you here and now.

"IF I STOP WORKING OUT, MY MUSCLES WILL TURN TO FLAB!"

This statement is the theme song of the Sour Grapes school of life, and to take it at face value would be ridiculous. Let me explain: Progress from a skinny or flabby frame to one of firm, taut muscles is a gradual, microscopic one, rooted deep within the muscle fibers. If you were to decide to take a break from your workout to sit on your duff or for whatever reason, the loss would occur just as gradually as the gains—even slower. But here's the bonus: Once you have worked your body to a certain point of fitness, getting back to that level after a long hiatus takes less effort than it did to achieve the original gains. For instance, if you've exercised and lifted weights for six months, improving cardiovascular and muscular health, and then you veg out in front of the TV for another six months, it would take only *three* months of work to bring you back to your initial level of fitness. "The muscles have memory," we say, and the cards are stacked in *your* favor.

"IT'S TOO LATE FOR ME, SO WHY BOTHER?"

This is not so much a myth as an expression of defeatism that can dog a man and interfere with progress, pleasure, and achievement all his life. When you think about it, isn't that statement perfectly crazy? Why sweep the floor when it'll just get dusty again? Why shower when I'll just have to do it again tomorrow morning? Each of us is unique, irreplaceable, and capable of the improvement we want and are willing to work for. Of course, some men are genetically gifted, born with a predisposition for a trim, muscular physique or have inherited muscular coordination or athletic ability. But everyone—and I mean *everyone*—has some quality, inherent or developed, that he can work on to optimal advantage. And these qualities are pleasures leading to other benefits, such as a natural inclination to achieve a toned body more easily.

"IT'S SO HARD . . ."

Perhaps the biggest and best-kept secret about making changes in your life regarding exercise and diet is how much *fun* it is. The myth has it that fitness requires hours of exhausting, grueling work, combined with hearty lashings of self-denial and sacrifice—no more bacon cheeseburgers with a double order of fries, an end to late-night pints of Häagen-Dazs in front of the TV. Well, to some guys this might indeed signal the end of happiness as they know it. But look at it another way: How about the pleasure of putting your body through its paces for an hour or so three times a week and feeling it capable of things you never thought it could do, seeing and feeling it firm up and strengthen? What's so bad about biting into a juicy peach or a hunk of fiery-red watermelon instead of a Krispy Kreme doughnut? And is late-night TV so much more of a treat than a bracing shower after an energetic game of volleyball, followed by dinner with your teammates? Even if we don't consider the very real pleasures of possessing a trimmer body, one that looks good both in clothes and out of them, the process of getting it that way can and should be seen as a delight rather than a burden and a chore. It's a matter of perspective—so maybe it's time to change yours and to see exercise, weight training, and healthy diet as their own reward.

"I'LL NEVER LOOK LIKE THAT . . ."

When I chose the photographs that illustrate this book, I had a specific intention: not to present near-impossible standards of beauty nor to make unrealistic promises about what my programs can do for you but to show you examples of men who, by exercising, weight training, and eating a

and available for three easy payments of stupidity. Do they work? Well, to some extent, and for some people (particularly those whose fitness level is a zero), yes, they can. But they require commitment and discipline, like any other lifestyle change. What good is a plastic shell intended to help you develop washboard abs if it takes up residence under your bed along with the dust bunnies and lost socks? And a ski machine can't help you increase your cardiovascular fitness if you use it primarily as a high-tech clothes rack. In other words, use these aids to exercise *as* exercise. It's not the manufacturer's fault if you get bored with your Glitz Glider and stop using it.

"I'M BIG BONED—I CAN'T HELP LOOKING THIS WAY." As I've said, to a certain extent we all have to live with genetic predispositions. But that doesn't mean we can't put up a fight: Just because your parents were overweight, you don't have to face the same fate. With a concerted effort you can change the way you look. If you're big boned (in our terms, a mesomorph), you can choose to upholster those massive bones with fat or with firm, taut muscle. Which would you rather have? It's entirely up to you.

"I DON'T WANT TO GET CAUGHT UP IN ALL THE VANITY." This is a central issue in fitness, and the question of vanity both defines and undermines all our ideas, preoccupations, and fears about the way we look. If beauty is, in fact, skin deep, then why should we care about the way we look? Well, for one thing, health is more than skin deep, and to the extent that we can influence our own well-being, fitness is certainly more than mere vanity. Psychologists distinguish between narcissism (an obsessive preoccupation with oneself) and healthy vanity, which speaks to our sense of self-image and the way in which we present ourselves to the world. Few things are less attractive than a preening, self-involved individual who doesn't seem able to pull himself away from the mirror. But someone who has worked hard on his physical package and who has an easy and comfortable attitude toward himself is more likely to accept others in just that way. That's the kind of person you want to be

healthy diet, have made themselves look the way they do. There are more than 40 different models—black, white, Asian, Native American—ranging in age from 22 to 45, each representing a different body type, a different look.

There is no single standard for male beauty; even Michelangelo's *David,* once taken as the classical ideal of the perfect male physique, has been reduced to a refrigerator magnet to be dressed up or down. The joke speaks to our anxieties about perfection and an idealized aesthetic: The truth is that we are less attracted to perfection than we realize, and that there are so many ways, whether you are an ectomorph, endomorph, or mesomorph, to make your body into something of which you can be proud and in which you can take pleasure.

GADGETS—DO THEY REALLY WORK? We've all seen the infomercials for machines, from plastic "Abdominators" to elaborate and expensive gym machines adapted for home use, all endorsed by smiling semi-celebrities

around. We're working toward self-acceptance and pleasure, not obsession and narcissism.

"MY PHYSICAL ABILITIES LIMIT ME." Guess what? Everyone has limitations. I'm not expecting to turn every reader of *Basic Training* into a Ironman triathelete or a bodybuilding finalist. But every man can improve his cardiovascular condition, build muscle, extend his flexibility, change the contours of his body, and learn a sport he can enjoy. Most important, everyone can take pleasure in feeling that he's improving his fitness level, adding fun to his daily routine and years to his life.

WHERE DO I FIT IN?

In a world filled with so many types of men of all shapes, sizes, and colors, each with his own appeal, fashion incorporates the evolution of the male form. As we enter the new millennium, what men wear is not merely pants and shirts, but what's under those pants and shirts. It's not enough to wear good-looking clothes; a man needs to look good under them. And getting beyond the whims of fashion and fad, it's not just the look of a toned, fit body that's so appealing—it is the way that level of health and development makes you feel.

There are three basic body types: ectomorph, endomorph, and mesomorph. Relatively few bodies are purely one type; most of us ex-

hibit the characteristics of two or even three types.

Mesomorph: Square and solid, with broad shoulders and narrow hips that are neither fat nor thin—these are the characteristics that define the mesomorph. Most men with this body type tend to make more accelerated muscular gains, increasing their strength and their size relatively quickly. John Travolta is a classic example: Possessed of rather slim, supple physique in *Saturday Night Fever,* he was trained by no less than Sylvester Stallone for his role as a buff dancer in *Staying Alive.* Other mesomorphs: Harrison Ford, Mel Gibson (again indicating striking physical changes this body is capable of), and Woody Harrelson.

Endomorph: Burly or husky describes the endomorphic individ-

ual, who tends to store more body fat than either of the other two. Their shape features rounder edges yet still maintains a strong and powerful stature. Dan Ackroyd, John Goodman, and Jay Leno are good examples of the endomorphic body type. Endomorphs need to be careful, but they can make extraordinary physical gains with proper diet and the right workout program.

Ectomorph: Long, lanky, and lean are good descriptive words for the ectomorphic type. This body's characteristics are typical of many swimmers and basketball players. With a solid weight-training program, the ectomorph will make strength gains and improve definition, but packing on bulk may be more difficult. Some examples: David Letterman, Brad Pitt, James

Woods, Michael "Kramer" Richards, Michael Jordan, and Dennis Rodman (obviously these last two are very highly developed ectomorphs, indicating the level of work to which you might aspire in your fitness, exercise, and diet routines).

The most difficult part of any lifestyle change is developing the motivation and direction we all require to get the results we want. The desire to look and feel good isn't enough. Getting to the point at which you can enjoy being fit requires more.

Men who take up a new activity in their spare time usually do so with a vengeance. They want to perfect their skills in a particular sport or hobby, and then proceed to excel at it. I believe that most of the drive comes from the ego. Nonetheless, a man can find great satisfaction in proving to himself that he in fact has the ability to learn and master a great task. It makes him feel like a champion, or even a king. This power is like a drug—it can intoxicate the most sober of men.

Living a fit lifestyle is more difficult than learning to play golf, shooting hoops, or taking part in a weekend league. These activities require our learning something very specific, and not really adjusting the way we have lived for years. This latter type of commitment affects all areas of our lives: socially, at work, in our relationships, at home, with our significant other, and, most important, with ourselves.

Basic Training can be your guide in offering you a new direction. It will dispel the myths about exercise and can help you put together a smart plan to get you moving. The images of the men in this book will allow you to see your own potential. These men may not necessarily be who you are, or even hope to be, but *you can* have the kind of body that you want through plain old hard work and discipline. We all need to start somewhere! Let this be your time to take action, and see yourself as strong, lean, and powerful. *Basic Training* is a holistic approach to a stronger body, a healthier way of life, and a more relaxed day-to-day existence.

10 REASONS TO BE FIT

1. You will feel better.

2. You will develop a healthy heart.

3. You will look stronger.

4. You will sleep better.

5. You will have a stronger sex drive.

6. You will have less fat on your body.

7. You will slow the aging process.

8. You will boost your immune system.

9. You will promote stronger bone density.

10. You will prove to yourself that you can do it.

Make a commitment contract to yourself and sign it. Take a piece of paper, write down your name and the date, and list a set of goals and desires about your fitness level that you would like to see happen. Give yourself a reasonable time frame and realistic objectives to achieve. By putting these down on paper, you may give yourself a clearer picture of the results you want.

CHAPTER TWO

Physical Education: P.E. 101

Before you embark on any physical fitness routine, it is vital that you understand who you are in terms that relate to the general population. Each of us is unique, but to tell a man who stands five foot two inches, at 185 pounds, that he can achieve the body of a swimmer six foot one and 175 pounds is silly and misleading.

This chapter will educate you about your body type and your current fitness level. Regard this as your personal starting point, a baseline from which you can reflect change and progress. This starting point not only reflects how you look but also assesses how you really feel: your activities, your diet, and your stress level, all of which contribute to how you function.

GET A CHECKUP

General questions regarding your health are also vital for making sure that your exercise program gets off to the right start. These questions may allow you to begin your journey in the best possible way, and give you the information which you probably know anyway.

1. Do you or does anyone in your family have a history of heart disease?

2. Do you have high blood pressure?

3. Are you diabetic?

4. Do you smoke cigarettes?

5. Have you had your cholesterol level tested recently?

6. Are you exercising currently?

None of these questions should deter you from exercise. They haven't been presented here to shame you or accuse you of anything. Before beginning any exercise program, you need to get a physical exam. Your doctor can determine whether or not exercise may put you at any risk. It is always a good idea to have some knowledge about your heart and lung capacity, your HDL and LDL ("good" and "bad" cholesterol levels). A knowledgeable doctor will reinforce your decision to begin a well-balanced fitness routine.

Newspapers, magazines, and books such as this one usually distinguish between "good" and "bad" cholesterol. HDL cholesterol is a component of healthy blood that carries oxygen freely to the muscles of the body and the brain. The LDL in blood is saturated with fat that clings to the walls of the blood-vessel system and major arteries of the heart. The lower the percentage of LDL cholesterol in your blood the better. The HDL blood acts like a drain cleaner scouring the fat buildup on arterial walls. Therefore the higher the percentage of HDL

cholesterol the better. You can reduce the LDL levels by reducing the
amount of fat you consume.

SELF-TESTING

A simple self-exam should be
thought of as preventive medicine. It
takes only a few minutes each
month, in the shower or bath or any
time you can get your hands on
things. I would suggest somewhere
private. Give yourself the time to be
thorough and uninterrupted. If you
feel something odd, such as an unusual growth or skin irritation, or
even something unusually sensitive,
check it out. Give it a couple days
and see if it changes. Don't be stub-
born, check it out.

BREAST CANCER

Just as women do, men should examine themselves for
breast cancer. There are roughly 1,500 cases of male breast
cancer reported each year in the United States, and the
number of cases is increasing every year. This disorder can
be as devastating to a man as it would be to a woman. All
the same rules apply, but because the attention to breast
cancer is primarily paid to women, men are often surprised to hear about it. Take a minute every month. Here's
what you should do: Raise your left arm. Take three or
four fingers of your right hand and explore the left pec
(breast) thoroughly. Beginning at the outer edge, press the
flat part of your fingers in small circular movements
around the pec. Gradually work toward the nipple. Be sure
you cover the entire pec. Pay special attention to the area
between the pec and the armpit. Feel for any lump or mass
under the skin. Anything unusual, discharge from the nip-

ple, for example, requires a doctor's attention. A friend of
mine detected his cancer while applying sunscreen at the
pool one summer. This effortless exam can save your life.

TESTICULAR EXAMINATIONS

Directly after a warm shower or bath, when the scrotum
is relaxed, roll your testicles between your fingers and
thumb. Notice any swelling, lumps, nodules, or a change
in consistency. Symptoms of testicular cancer include a
change in the consistency of the testis and/or an enlargement of one testis. If there is anything unusual or notice-
able, consult your physician.

PROSTATE EXAMINATION: 10 SECONDS FELT AROUND THE WORLD

Cancer of the prostate: the words no man wants to hear. About 122,000 new cases develop every year in the United States. The problem of detecting prostate cancer is that it may cause no symptoms; late in the course of the disease, obstructions, pain, and blood in the urine may occur.

So how can you protect yourself? Simple: Have your primary-care physician check your prostate at your regular physical exam. This should take place once a year for men over 50, every other year for men over 40, and regularly for men in their 20s and 30s. The procedure itself is no big deal, about ten seconds of discomfort as the doctor has you lean over the examining table and inserts a gloved and lubricated finger into the rectum to check for enlargement of the prostate or any obstruction. And that's it. Also taken at this time is a blood sample, because elevated prostate-specific antigen (PSA) levels in the blood may indicate prostate enlargement or malignancy. Treatment for prostate cancer includes surgery, radiation therapy, and hormone-control therapy, and the cure rate is encouraging. So don't ignore your prostate—have it checked regularly.

WHY GET FIT?

This question is a roadblock we set up for ourselves not to exercise. You have heard the answers so many times. Men who enjoy exercise believe in themselves and want to build healthier bodies to take them throughout their lives, with the energy and physiological benefits that happen because of exercise.

INCREASE MUSCLE STRENGTH. Strong muscles help you move with ease and without restriction. Muscle will help you to stand with flawless posture, ultimately ensuring your spine a healthier existence. Building muscle will also boost your metabolism and burn fat from your body, creating a leaner shape.

IMPROVE HEART AND LUNGS. Building the strength of the heart will create a more efficient muscle, pumping more blood with less effort and with less stress. Like any other machine, when all the parts are taken care of, the heart will run with ease. The lungs provide you with oxygen needed to stay alive. Keeping your lungs in optimal health will ensure the most oxygen delivery to the brain and the blood.

BECOME MORE FLEXIBLE. Flexibility reduces the risk of injury; helps release muscle tension and soreness; promotes better movement around joints, which will allow freedom for better posture; and offers mental and physical relaxation. With training, just as with weights or aerobics, you can improve the flexibility in all the muscles of your body, at any age. The only limitations are genetic ones; each person (man or woman) has the capacity to stretch within his or her range of motion.

IMPROVE THE DENSITY OF BONES. There are 206 bones in your body, and they are alive. Many people think that after a certain point our bones stop changing and stay hard like chalk. Well, think again. The bone is composed of collagen, an organic complex protein, and an inorganic component of mineral salts, mainly calcium and phosphorous. Bones constantly change throughout your life. Bone is capable of adjusting its strength in proportion to the stress placed upon it (Wolff's Law). If stresses such as weight training, walking, running, or aerobic training are put on bone over a period of time, bones will become more dense through increased collagen and mineral salts, delivered by blood and nutrition. If bone is not stressed, it will become less dense, and eventually the organic complex proteins, minerals, and other matter can be withdrawn. This happens primarily with sedentary people.

IMMUNE-SYSTEM RESPONSE. By starting an exercise program you will boost your immune system to help ward off viruses and dispense healthful nutrients to the entire body. As you exercise aerobically, the white blood cells, including the T-helper cells (lifeguards), are swept back into circulation where they function at maximum overdrive. This is called demargination, and when

achieved will last for hours. Exercise will also cause you to sweat, which in itself is a cleanser.

Breathing and muscle contractions open the lymph nodes and maintain a healthy flow throughout the body, relieving any blockage that might occur in the system. Sweating will also rid your body of toxins and waste products through the sweat glands. It is important that you wash after a workout session to cleanse your body of the impurities that are pumped to the surface of your skin in the form of sweat.

FAT VERSUS LEAN: AM I FAT?

What is fat and what is lean? A common myth is that if you weigh less than your typical body type, you must have less fat. This is not necessarily true. You can weigh 150 pounds and still be considered obese. It all depends on how much lean mass you have on your body. This often confuses people because they look thin to themselves in the mirror, but statistically, because a thin person's body fat level can exceed "ideal" percentages, that same person could be distinguished as obese.

WHAT THE SCALE DOESN'T TELL YOU

At sometime in your life, at the doctor, at the gym, or even at a carnival or state fair, you have stepped on a scale to check out what your body weighs. Relying on the scale to give you positive reinforcement is another thing entirely. Try keeping the information the scale is telling you in perspective. The best thing to do is to understand the difference between fat and lean muscle mass (muscle).

A scale simply measures the weight of your entire body in pounds or kilograms. The scale cannot separate the muscles, bones, blood, and internal organs from fat. The separation of lean mass and fat is called body composition; the ratio ultimately determines your body fat percentage and will be kinder and ultimately offer you better information, information that you can use rather

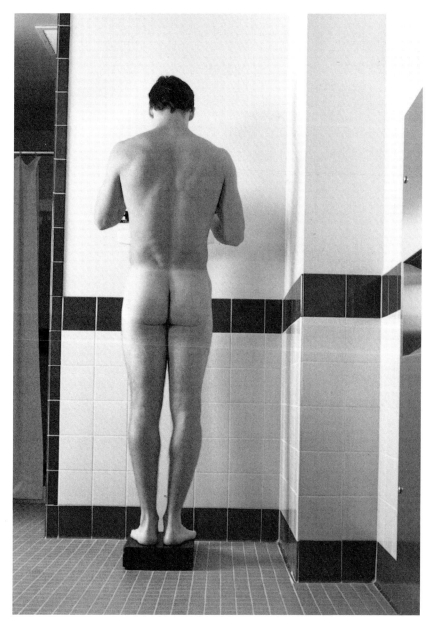

yourself by the digit on the scale. The scale can be misleading and cruel.

Scenario: You have decided to start an exercise program after a few years of sitting at the job and in front of your computer. This is a good choice, so you start by lifting weights a few times a week and doing some moderate aerobic exercise four or five times a week. Research suggests that, combined with a balanced diet and a good attitude, this regimen offers the possibility of losing one to two pounds of fat per week.

This change in your daily routine would help you to lose about ten pounds of fat in about three months. However, with your strength-training program you have developed muscle, which has increased your body weight by about three pounds, a very good change. If the scale were the only measurement of your success, it would show only seven pounds lost, therefore giving you the wrong information and robbing you of the reassurance you need to continue.

Because fat takes up so much space, with that same 10-pound loss you would see smaller measurements around your hips, stomach, and upper legs. The best way to judge the success of a weight-loss program is to pay attention to the way your clothes fit. Think about it. Your clothes are the first indication of weight gain, so look to the same source for praise. Your clothes will tell you the truth and so will a mirror. You know your body, and you know when you are storing a little extra baggage. Look at yourself in the mirror without judgment and see your changes. They will happen as long as you show up and do the work. If you went solely by the scale,

than just a banal digit that seems only to defeat those seeking reinforcement.

Focusing on the number can be a problem because you don't know how much of that digit is fat and how much is the rest of you. Muscle weighs more than fat. Muscle is dense, like a piece of chocolate fudge, and fat is like whipped cream; it takes a lot of whipped cream to equal the weight of a small piece of chocolate fudge. Really, if you take one pound of fat and one pound of muscle you would see the amount of each separately is very different than their equal weight. Try not to rate

you might be tempted to quit. Increasing muscle mass not only helps you become stronger—making your daily chores easier—muscle also expends calories all day long, even when you are at rest. Over time, the added pounds of muscle can help you burn thousands of additional calories, make your physique look strong, and boost your self-image.

There is some basic information you should have regarding metabolism and fat storage systems that may help you understand the process by which you may assess everything that you eat, as well as the importance of a complete exercise regimen.

For men, the ideal range of body fat is between 12 and 18 percent of body weight. This simply means that if you weigh 170 pounds, 20 to 30 pounds of entire body weight is made up of fat. That is the goal area, the healthy range. This is what you should be striving for through diet, exercise, a flexibility routine, and stress-relieving techniques.

Fat loss will reduce the risks of cardiovascular disease, cancer, diabetes, and other health dangers while encouraging longevity and a better self-image.

PINCH YOURSELF!

This simple test may, of course, be done in private. Three areas of the body will be tested, and the results will give you a self-analysis of your body's own composition; that is, the percentages of lean muscle and fat that make up your body. Organs, bones, and fluid help tilt the scales too, but you should be most concerned about the per-

centage of the body that is fat. Keep in mind that body weight fluctuates by several pounds over the course of a typical day. This fluctuation is primarily due to the amount of water in your body. If you weigh yourself before and after a rigorous workout session, you may find that you've lost a few pounds. Actually, it's just water loss.

Three areas to self-test are the front of the thigh, midway between your knee and your hip and slightly off center; your waist line; and your midback. If it's difficult to get at your back, an alternative spot, either the pec or the tricep, will do, but the back will give you a better

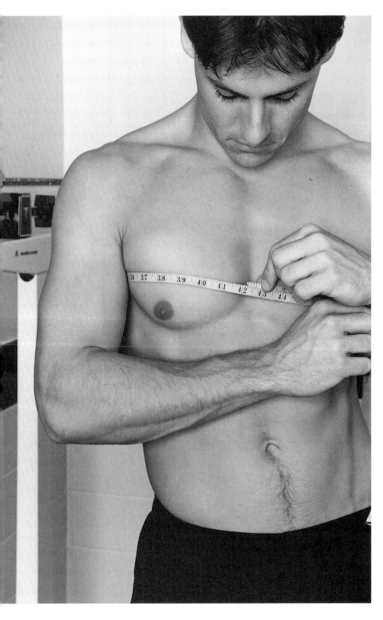

Measure your waist, chest, legs, hips, and buttocks and record the number somewhere. Joining an exercise program will affect the digits recorded months from now and give you positive acknowledgment of your work.

STRENGTH, FLEXIBILITY, AND ENDURANCE

I have always hated tests. I tend to predict the results and sell myself short by second guessing, and believe that "they" are out to trick or humiliate me. Testing your fitness level is completely different, but the results can channel the same type of defeatist reaction that would turn a man away from fitness forever.

Think of this time as the starting line, the place where you are right now. You have to have an idea of where you are in order to realize that you have made changes in your body and your life. These simple-to-follow tests have no passing grade; you cannot fail! They are positions that show you your current level of fitness targeting three components. After you have completed each position or set of maximal repetitions, write the number of reps and the level of difficulty on a piece of paper and hold onto it. You might want to look back one day and praise yourself for the advances that you will have made.

These fitness tests will show you where your weak points are and how you can then choose your best course of action. You do have a choice here; I am just trying to lead you to making the right choice: the "fitness" choice.

TESTING

The most effective exercises to determine your current level of strength are the push-up and the crunch. For the purposes of a home workout environment, I am using these exercises because they can be performed by most everyone and they test your upper and middle body.

Whether in gym class or boot camp, the push-up is performed with your legs fully extended, toes on the floor;

result. This is not a scientific test by any means, but it does give you the opportunity to pinch yourself all over and to see exactly where you do store fat.

Pinch each of these areas by taking an inch of skin or so and pinching it until you feel you can pull away from your frame. The amount of the skin fold that your fingers holds is what is *FAT.* If the amount is substantial then you have some work to do. You get to be the judge and the jury, but you shouldn't think of punishment or a sentence; change the words to encouragement and incentive.

Another method would be measuring your waist with a tape: a plain measuring tape from your bachelor's sewing kit sitting in the drawer; yardsticks don't work.

keep the middle of your body tight like a plank and your hands firmly planted on the floor. The push-up will use multiple muscles in order to perform even one repetition. This single exercise will give an overall idea of the strength of your upper body versus your lower body. Testing will give you a ground-level digit, a baseline number to start from. The lower body participates in more daily functions than the upper body, and we realize that the legs are very powerful muscles themselves, so this test is primarily designed to estimate the strength capacity for the upper part of the body.

For testing purposes it will be necessary to lump you into groups according to your age, which can be painful to the most sensitive, but this is where age has its benefits. There are tests prescribed by the President's Council on Physical Fitness, the American Heart Association, the American Council on Exercise, and the American College of Sports Medicine, to name just a few. To attempt all the tests would be difficult and time-consuming. You just need a starting ground, a few simple tests that will provide you with the same information as the others.

STRENGTH TEST: THE POWER OF 1

Push-ups are the most effective exercises to determine your strength level. Perform as many as you can without losing your body position or technique. It is important that you find out your strength level in order to choose the right weight for you to use for your program. Lay down on the floor, face down, and bring your hands directly below your shoulders. Push yourself off the floor; that is 1. Go. Record the results in a notebook.

I am not giving you a list of averages. If after two weeks of training with the Basic Training exercises you are able to perform more, then you have succeeded. You will also have a record of your starting place. If in the test you are unable to do any push-ups, use a light weight to begin your routine. If you are able to do 20 push-ups, then you can start out with about 10 pounds for dumbbells and a 20- to 30-pound barbell. More than that you can determine on your own.

I know I said no averages, then I thought about it. Men need averages to estimate and prove to themselves

MEASURING FITNESS IN PUSH-UPS

AGE	NUMBER OF PUSH-UPS PERFORMED				
15–29	UP TO 20	21–34	35–44	45–55	55+
30–39	UP TO 15	15–24	25–34	35–44	44+
40–49	UP TO 12	12–19	20–29	30–39	39+
OVER 50	UP TO 8	8–14	15–24	25–34	34+
	VERY LOW	LOW	MODERATE	HIGH	VERY HIGH

MEASURING FITNESS IN CRUNCHES

AGE	NUMBER OF CRUNCHES PERFORMED			
15–19	12	25	46	75
20–29	15	25	47	75
30–39	17	28	56	75
40–49	24	35	70	75
50–59	15	25	52	74
60+	6	12	30	53
	BELOW AVERAGE	AVERAGE	ABOVE AVERAGE	EXCELLENT

where they fit in. That is okay, but I think you should measure against yourself so that you can include self-esteem into the equation. Don't let the numbers rule. Tell yourself about how strong you are and add some reassurance about what you want to become.

The same will apply to your midsection and the strength of your abdominal muscles. Turn over and do as many crunches as you can without stopping. Come up only halfway, just until your shoulder blades lift off the floor, and then down again. Keep your hands at your side and let them slide past your hips as you lift. You should be able to pace yourself to perform about 25 crunches per minute. If you surpass 75 crunches, you have great strength in your midsection. Every number here is important. Record and strive for that number again and surpass it every time. After a certain amount of time you will be doing more than you thought you ever could. If numbers aren't your thing, just lay down and crunch for your own sake, trust me.

FLEXIBILITY TEST:
SENSE AND FLEXIBILITY

This test is simple enough and will show you how important it is to start stretching right now. Just sit on the floor with your legs extended in front of you. Sit tall enough so you feel your chest lift up and your shoulders stack over your hips. This position may already feel painful behind the legs; if so, you are in desperate need of a stretching routine of some kind. Put your hands on the floor beside your hips and slide your hands along your legs to your knees on the floor if possible. If you can do this maintaining your posture, your flexibility level isn't too bad. If you can go past your knees, your level of flexibility is good. Record how far you were able to reach beyond your knees and try it again when you test your strength (push-ups) in a couple weeks.

Turn onto your stomach and lie flat on the floor. Bring your arms under your head. Bend at your knee and bring one foot toward your buttocks. If this is easy for you, grasp your foot with your hand. You will feel the stretch in the front of your thigh. If you are having a hard time even bending at the knee, you now know that you need a stretching program. Record how far you were able to stretch—and be honest. You have to stretch daily in order to stretch more the next time, so get going.

ENDURANCE TEST:
DANCING AS FAST AS I CAN!

There are several ways to test your endurance, or how fit your heart is. The test for you to perform without the luxury of a treadmill, a running track, or a walk outside is a step test. You will need a platform that measures 12 inches from the floor. Keep in mind that it should be sturdy and wide enough for your foot. A cadence of about 96 beats per minute is necessary to establish how quickly you should step up and down. You could use a song such as "What's Love Got to Do with It?" by Tina Turner or "Freedom" by George Michael to give you the right beat. Step up and down for about a minute to warm up and rehearse the step technique. Set an egg timer or a

PULSE RATE

AGE	BEATS PER MINUTE AFTER 3 MINUTES OF AEROBIC EXERCISE			
18–25	117–120	100–105	79–90	79
26–35	118–128	100–107	81–89	81
36–45	120–130	104–112	83–96	83
46–55	123–132	106–116	87–97	87
56–65	121–129	104–112	86–97	86
over 65	121–130	104–113	88–96	88
	POOR	AVERAGE	GOOD	EXCELLENT

stopwatch for three minutes and then begin. After three minutes, stop, sit down, and take your pulse at either the radial (wrist) or carotid (neck) pulse point. Record the number and then take your pulse again after a minute. This will also determine your recovery heart rate. The faster your heart restores itself to a normal heart rate, the more efficiently it is working. The chart above will help you determine your results.

Keep your records and put them into your logbook or on the fridge. Pull out these statistics at a later time and see how you've improved. I think you will be pleasantly surprised, but only if you work for results. If you don't, then the numbers will stay the same and so will you. In fact, if you don't start, your numbers only go down with time. Don't let this happen; get started now.

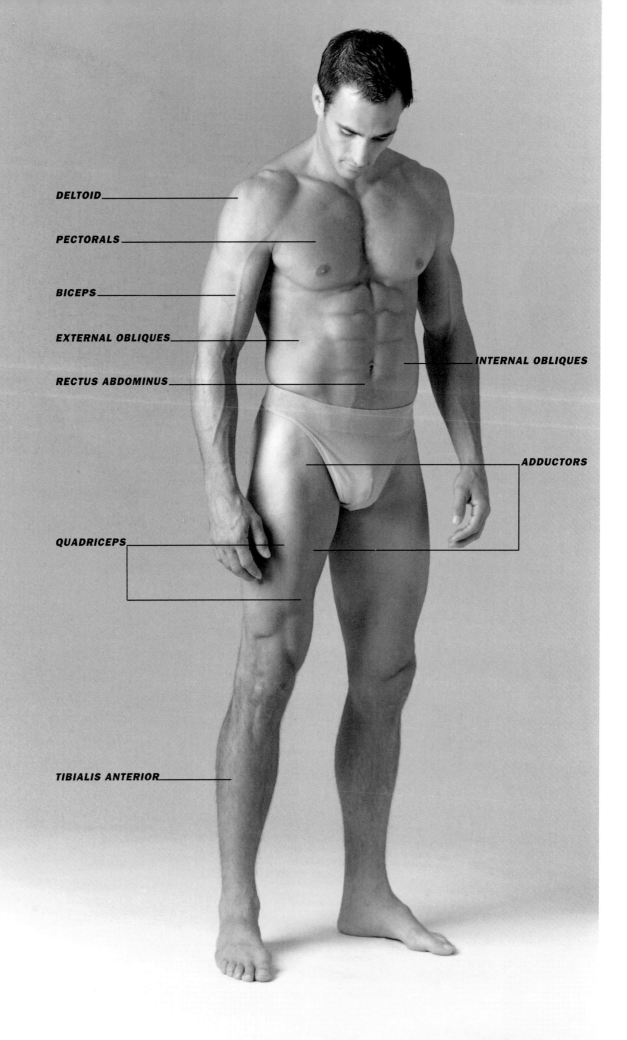

DELTOID

PECTORALS

BICEPS

EXTERNAL OBLIQUES

INTERNAL OBLIQUES

RECTUS ABDOMINUS

ADDUCTORS

QUADRICEPS

TIBIALIS ANTERIOR

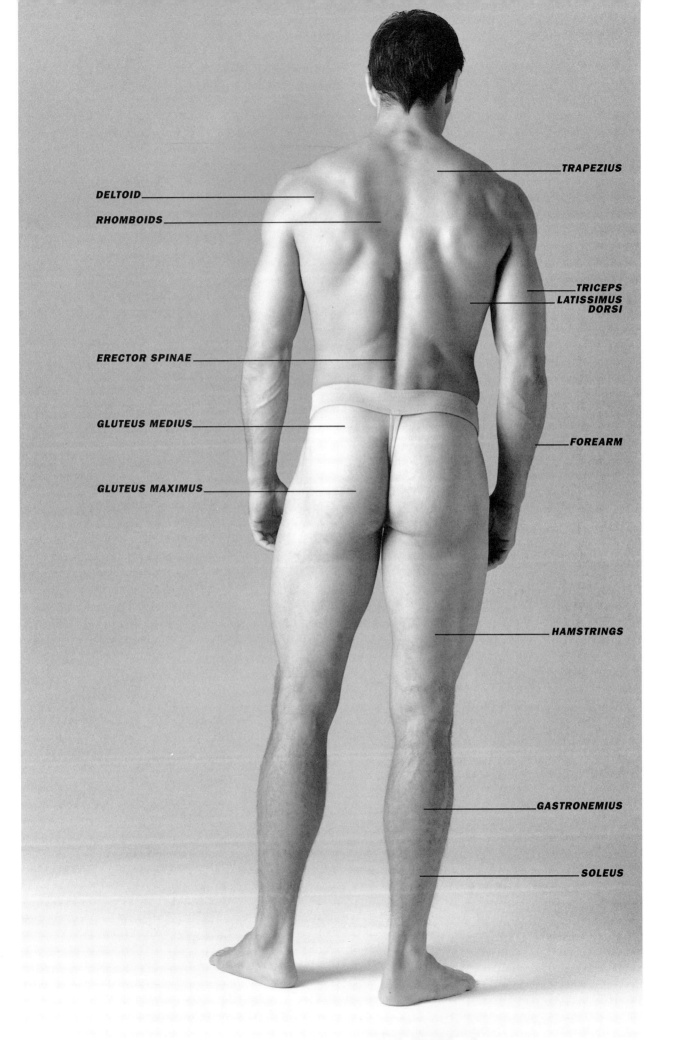

TRAPEZIUS

DELTOID

RHOMBOIDS

TRICEPS
LATISSIMUS
DORSI

ERECTOR SPINAE

GLUTEUS MEDIUS

FOREARM

GLUTEUS MAXIMUS

HAMSTRINGS

GASTRONEMIUS

SOLEUS

GETTING STARTED

Getting started is always the most difficult part of this entire regimen. Just standing there, wondering what to do and how many times to do it is often the reason so many people stop prematurely with a fitness program. First, you need to find out how strong in fact you are from the beginning. This can be a considerably humbling experience. Humility never killed anyone, and it should only fuel your enthusiasm. Second, you need to test your flexibility. This component is as important as strength! Third, the most important factor of all is learning the preliminary limits of your individual aerobic capacity. The heart and lungs need to be strengthened as much as your biceps and quadriceps. Aerobic exercise is the key to a complete workout program. There are several ways for you to exercise your heart and lungs which will be suggested later in this chapter.

It is very important for you to understand the components that make up a balanced program, a course that will lead you to success and a healthier future. These components are:

1. aerobic training
2. weight training
3. flexibility (stretching)
4. diet
5. rest (recovery)
6. adaptation (change)
7. intensity

AEROBIC TRAINING

Aerobic fitness (cardiovascular fitness) is created by raising one's heart rate to an appropriate and safe level, and then maintaining that rate for a certain period of time. Of course, this is greatly dependent upon one's age. The charts in P. E. 101 will help you determine your "target" heart rate. To increase your cardiovascular fitness level, attempt to maintain moderate activity for a period of at least 20 minutes a day. The more time put in, the

quicker the gains and the sooner you'll begin to see a real change.

There are many claims out there about getting fit in "only" three minutes a day. Such claims will only benefit someone who has never walked on his own two feet at any time in his entire life. If you ask anyone with any knowledge of the body, he will tell you that such a promise is a hoax, invented solely to sell you still another product for just three easy payments of stupidity!

What we need to remember is that the time that we invest in our workouts and change of lifestyle is an investment in being a healthier individual. Creating a balance is like orchestrating music. The components, like instruments, must support one another, but must work independently (solo) as well as in combination (in concert).

WEIGHT TRAINING

Weight training (resistance training) involves exercises that use the skeletal muscles (quadriceps, biceps, etc.) to push and pull a weight that will cause an overload to the muscle. Be it your own body weight, a dumbbell, a machine, or a rock, muscle needs to work against something to gain strength. By lifting and stretching the muscles, causing them to exhaust and then to recover, the tissue gets stronger for the next time it has to perform a similar task. By repeating the process, the muscle systems get stronger and change their size and structure. However, allowing your muscles to recover is vital to strength building.

Weight training evolves when you progressively increase the workload the muscles push or pull against each time they adapt to the prior load. There is a chain reaction going on here: muscle stimulation through exercise, change through rest and recovery, and continued stimulation by intensity variations of exercise.

FLEXIBILITY (STRETCHING)

Stretching is as important a component of a complete fitness routine as lifting weights regularly or running on a treadmill to burn fat and exercise your heart and lungs.

Oftentimes, when beginning a workout session, men will pass over the stretch and get right to the work; they want to get their work finished and leave. In many ways the stretch is similar to the foreplay before great sex; preparation and getting into the heat of it makes it better. Your muscle systems need to prepare for the heavy work required by exercise; stretching increases the mobility of the joints and soothes aching muscle tissue. Stretching will assist in the release of lactic acids from the muscle surface, allowing the body to absorb the chemical, getting rid of the "burn" you may feel in the muscle when it is stressing.

Flexibility training will keep your muscle tissue supple and smooth. Think of your body as a system of miraculous elastic strips, running diagonally, vertically, and around the skeleton. The elastic man has the ability to shorten and lengthen these bands within his own limits or boundaries. If the bands are shortened only, they will stay short and tight and hold all the bone close to the center. By lengthening the bands, they stay flexible and stretch with ease, but they need to be pulled to a set point, not overstretched, so that the blood can flow and the acids that build up on the muscle can be released.

Stretching provides you with two variables that men seldom think about, but I think they are vital and important to bring up. Stretching your muscles is like maintaining a car; if you don't change the oil, rotate the tires, and check out the suspension, your car will drive like a tank. Maintaining flexibility will also help in the prevention of injuries or assist the rehabilitation of ones that already exist.

Pulling yourself open, which in blunt terms is what you are doing when you stretch, also opens you up, spreads you out so that you can relax your body and your brain.

DIET

There's no end of books out there that will tell you the best way to eat, the best diet of the moment, outrageous plans that make incredible claims of magic weight loss, and starvation routines that can actually damage your body and its digestive system. This component of the healthy fitness regimen would prescribe a low-fat diet that would supply the body with the proper amount of energy to perform the exercises you choose, maintain an active daily life, and supply your body with the natural vitamins and nutrients to maintain strong muscles and bones. The key to a balanced diet that will offer your the rewards of weight loss or weight gain, whichever you choose, is to keep the amount of fat to a minimum.

REST (RECOVERY)

Resting between exercise sessions is an exercise in itself. How hard you are working, and with what intensity, will determine how much recovery your body needs to repair and adapt. Without proper rest periods your body ends up overtraining, resulting in exhaustion or injury. There are many men who compete with themselves; they overachieve and believe that more is more and that rest seems like a waste of time. Rest can also imply lazy. The fact is that your body needs a certain amount of rest in order to perform better the next time. The problem with working out is that some men will work out to total exhaustion, and then give up completely.

For many, this component requires trial and error. You will have to monitor when you feel you have rested a body part enough, or if your intensity level is such that you need a couple days away from working the same body part again. Rest can take many forms. You don't have to rest lying down—take a walk, sit in the park, do something else.

ADAPTATION (CHANGE)

When your muscle system has perfected a method of training, and the reaction has been noted in strength advances, or by stretching a little longer through the hamstring, your muscles have adapted to the workload. The same holds true for the heart and the lungs; after a certain period of time they also work more efficiently and with less effort. That means your fitness level has increased and you are a fitter person than you were before you started: You have adapted. After a while, however, your body will have the knowledge that you have carefully and skillfully applied to it and the body will start to work in an automated state. The body knows how much effort it requires to get the same job done; the muscle knows how hard it will have to work until it gets tired like the last time. You will see and feel the changes in your physique and your stamina level off and stay at the same level. After a period of time, your body will work automatically.

Once you achieve a certain level, stay there for a couple of weeks and then change the routine, the sequence of exercise, or try another type of program entirely. You will see and feel a response in your body the way you did when you first started training.

INTENSITY

Intensity is judged by the person participating in the exercise itself. How hard you push or pull is truly up to you, but to commit to change you have to reach a point where the last repetition you perform in a set is the last one you could possibly do without compromising your form and losing the central position. The term is *working to failure*. Sounds a little negative to me, but other men will know what you are talking about when you mention it.

Working to this point of failure in both aerobic training and weight training has a positive and negative outcome. With aerobic training, the intensity should be set at a moderate level and sustained for a set period of time. If the intensity level were set to

a failure point, you would run as fast as you can, for as long as you can. Not a good idea! Bursts of energy with regard to aerobic training are safe and effective, as is the case with interval training or circuit training, but the intensity during aerobic conditioning should stay moderate.

Weight training requires failure to occur in order to judge the intensity of the workload or weight. This is what your muscles crave and that is where strength is found. Adjustments are always appropriate for every goal you set for yourself. If you are just starting out, you might want to keep the weights light and learn the exercises and technique. That would be a great start and you would get the benefits promised for that level. If you have been away from exercise for a while, you could intensify more quickly because your body has muscle memory and you have the technical information already, although you should remember that muscle will respond as it did once before, so you be the judge.

Listen to your body; it will tell you what is going on and what you should do. If the weight is too heavy or if you have done too many repetitions, put the weight down before you drop it. Never compromise technique for weight. Be aware that your form and focus, combined with your own motivational drive, will successfully reward you with the results you desire.

STARTING POINT

Set yourself up with the appropriate exercises by testing each of the components stated above, and then move on. It is necessary to know how many repetitions should be performed with each exercise and stretch, and how long you should exercise aerobically. These tests may also help you to determine your "perceived exertion." This is a subjective judgment you make as to how hard you are working. Keeping your heart rate in the target 60 to 90 percent (or the 50 to 80 percent) range is the ultimate goal. It is best to take your heart rate (pulse) numerous times so that you can judge realistically how you are doing.

CHAPTER THREE

Preparation

TRADE TOOLS

Getting set up is a workout in itself. Some men need every toy, every gizmo and state-of-the-art garment to enhance their workout technique and attitude, but others can get the best workout in their life just by tying their shoes and getting into it. We all have our own ways of doing things and the same goes with getting a fitness program under way. Initially you may find that the equipment you have is fine and will serve you quite well. I can get a great workout using any chair or park bench, dunes and gravel roads, big rocks and tree branches. Realistically speaking, we are concerned for this moment with the home workout. Below you will find a list of things you might find useful if you intend to put this book to work for you.

EQUIPMENT LIST FOR HOME WORKOUT

1. Depending on the type of floor surface you have in the space you are working out in, it might be a good idea to have a mat or towel available for padding. A hardwood floor can get uncomfortable against the spine, and if you're sweating, a mat or towel will absorb moisture.

2. Benches can be very useful and are easily available. In a sporting-goods store you can purchase a sturdy metal bench or a step that is used in step aerobic classes. Many of these steps are too small, so make sure yours is at least 4 feet long. The risers underneath can elevate the step to 8 or 12 inches off the floor. These are lightweight and easy to store. Unless you have a room dedicated to exercise, a bench becomes part of the furniture. Chairs can be used to support the body for certain exercises, but they can be a little shaky if they aren't the right size. If you are using a chair, get one with a wide seat, straight back, and no arms. Avoid chairs with fabric on the seat.

3. Hand weights or dumbbells. If you are buying a set of hand weights, I suggest the kind with interchangeable plates on a short grip. This type of dumbbell requires a clip or collar to hold the plates on the end of the handle. For safety reasons make sure the collar fits and tightens easily. Different exercises require different weights at every level of your program and development. So it might be a good idea to invest in a good set of dumbbells from the start. I would suggest 5, 10, and 15 pounds to start with if you are buying individual dumbbells. Having several sets of independent hand weights (3, 5, 8, 10, 12, 15, 20, 22.5, 25 pounds) is costly and takes up a lot of space. A single set of interchangeable weights can give you all the weight you need, and you can add on when the time is right. There are magnets available that you can stick onto the end of a dumbbell to increase the weight of each dumbbell by 1¼ to 2½ pounds, without the steep cost to you.

4. Gloves. There are many types of gloves that can be worn while lifting weights. Different materials can provide better comfort while lifting iron and also reduce the size of the calluses on your palms. Some of the materials used include leather, cotton mesh, neoprene, or stretch nylon. All of these materials are good and should be decided on by personal taste and comfort. They will help reduce the risk of dropping the weights you are lifting and give you more confidence during your set.

5. Weight-lifting belts can reduce the risk of many lower back injuries and help promote better lifting technique. There are a variety of belts to choose from: they come in different widths and materials. Make sure to choose one that will give you a few inches to tighten the belt when necessary. Not only will these notches stabilize your lower back, but they will also record your progress: as you tighten the belt a notch you should notice that you have lost a few inches off your waist. Two benefits in one.

Allow the belt to dry out and keep it as clean as possible. Sweat may make leather brittle and will definitely make nylon smell. The belt can be used for all exercises for a period of time while you're learning the techniques. Try to graduate to relying on your abdominal strength to act as your stabilizer. When you are lifting very heavy weight, a belt is highly recommended.

6. Good shoes can make a big difference in the way you work out. Aerobic activities require your feet to be comfortable and well supported. Cross trainers provide you with most of the support you will need for aerobic activities and weight training. If you are sold on a single aerobic activity, shop for a shoe specifically built for the activity you have in mind. Make sure the shoes have good arch and ankle support, and

don't let advertising and fashion dictate to you—listen to your feet.

Try on several pairs of shoes, making sure that there is a thumb's width between the tip of your longest toe and the end of the shoe. The arch support should meet your arch exactly. When you find those shoes that are right for you, put them on and get going.

High tops—great for basketball and other sports in which you stop and pivot quickly. The rapid change in direction puts stress on the ankle joint, and the added support of a high top is important.

Low rise—a good running or walking shoe and a classic all-purpose sneaker. Whether it is made of fabric or leather determines the weight of the shoe, so if you want a lightweight, stick with the canvas. Many of these shoes are also washable, so they will look as good too.

Mesh inserts make shoes lighter and help keep your feet dry by letting the sweat evaporate. Think of your feet as being steamed like a vegetable; the mesh may help the steam escape more easily.

SET UP A LOG

Measure your progress by keeping a journal or a log. All you need is an inexpensive notebook and a pen, and a little honesty. Those fancy "personal organizers" bound in Moroccan leather or Peruvian calfskin cost more than a pair of top-of-the-line cross trainers and can be as intimidating as membership in a state-of-the-art gym. Sometimes less is more, and I think that this is the case with logbooks. You are really the only one who will see the thing, unless you lose it, in which case the whole world will know.

Start with a line or two in the notebook. Write down the date, the activity, and how long your session was. Let's say you were on a treadmill. You stayed with a moderate-intensity walk for 25 minutes. You stretched your legs and shoulders before and after. So your log entry might look like this:

10/17/98 Treadmill 25 min (mod intensity)

For weight training, write down the date, the muscles you are working, how many reps, and how many sets. Did you stretch? I am not letting up on the stretching thing! Men never get enough stretching into their workouts. They still carry that caveman mentality of lifting big rocks and then going home. Stretching will prepare you mentally and physically and keep you from suffering through bouts of muscle ache and, even more important, injury.

Keep the log simple. It's enough that you're doing the work without the additional task of turning every workout into a novel. But your log can keep you moti-vated and focused. There is less chance for you to slow down or get sidetracked if you are keeping tabs on your own workout and you can see in black and white the progress you're making. This progress doesn't have to (and shouldn't) be dramatic—just steady. Make your log entries a daily or three-times-weekly acknowledgment of a positive experience, the written proof of your commitment to a healthy life.

Flip ahead to the back of the notebook and write down your goals: Where do you want to be a month from now? Let's say you want to be taking three long walks a week—a reasonable goal. Maybe you think after a couple of weeks that those walks might get boring. But you worry that three runs might prove too difficult and that you'll get discouraged. Fine—just write down "Three cardiovascular things (the technical term) a week." One of them could be a lunchtime workout or walk. Or you could decide to walk home briskly from the office, translating a 15-minute bus ride into an invigorating walk. And there are so many variations: steps ups on a park bench, lunges in a lobby, bike riding, dogwalking, Frisbeeing—even taking the stairs instead of the elevator in your apartment building (someone we know began a fitness program by putting a load of laundry into the basement washing machine and spent the 30 minutes of the cycle walking up and down the stairs). And you can always walk, anywhere. Seen this way, exercise isn't something you have to dress for; it's a come-as-you-are, casual, natural part of your everyday routine.

SPACE: THE FITNESS FRONTIER

For anyone wanting to begin a fitness program, no space is too small: a tiny meat-and-potatoes gym, a neighborhood playground, the corner of a studio apartment. But for those who don't really want to commit to a program, no space is big enough—not the flossiest state-of-the-art club, not a public park, not a spacious den, not a private spa overlooking the Grand Canyon. How much space you need is relative: If you're really motivated, you can fill liquid-detergent bottles with sand and use them as weights, or do step-ups on a kitchen chair—in your own kitchen, or "stair-climb" at 3:00 a.m. in your apartment building stairwell. If you're defeated and defeatist, you'll find reasons to hunker down with an Agatha Christie or Ken Follett novel at a gorgeous country home with a fully equipped gym, pool, and landscaped running paths.

So really, it's up to you: Environment is absolutely no barrier to a healthy way of life.

HOME VERSUS CLUB: YOUR CHOICE

The choice of home or club as your place to work out is entirely up to you; each has advantages and drawbacks.

At home you have privacy and complete control of your fitness routine. You can exercise at any time of the day or night, you don't have to share equipment or "work in" with anyone else, and you pay no fees or membership dues. You can begin your day with a workout, exercise just before bedtime, or schedule yourself for an afterwork session. With a modest outlay for weights, an exercise mat, maybe even an adjustable bench, you'll have outfitted a completely functional home gym. And you don't have to drag yourself out of the house or apartment on a cold, rainy day to get to the gym—you're already there.

At a club, exercise is the main event. "I'm going to

the gym," men announce, and they're indicating more than their destination. The club beckons, and you can leave your troubles and worries, the unpaid bills and family strife at the door, because the moment you step in, you know why you're there. This time is for you—no one else. And the gym is a playground, offering you the kind of freedom you haven't had since you were a kid, the joy in physical activity you may remember from school recess. It's been said that the health club may just be the new temple or church for the millennium: a center for socializing and physical and spiritual renewal and growth, whether it's tucked away on a city street or the toast of a suburban strip mall. And it's the place to inspire your own ambitions and goals, because you'll always see people more and less advanced than you; it's the perfect environment in which to find motivation, pleasure, and satisfaction in your fitness program.

Someone I know says, "No matter how bad things are, no matter how terrible my day or my checkbook balance is, I always feel better after I've been to the gym." The effort invariably pays off—in physical well-being, in satisfaction of having met a goal, and in the knowledge that you can go to the gym any time for a surge in energy, self-confidence, and fun.

TIME IS ON YOUR SIDE

When is the best time to exercise? The answer: Whenever you'll do it. What's good for you? Are you up with the birds and raring to meet the day? If so, you might want to schedule an early-morning workout, whether at home or at the club. Then you can shower, shave, dress, and launch yourself into your day.

But what if it takes you ages to wake up, and you're really not at your mental (let alone physical) peak until, say, 2:00 p.m.? You might want to come home after work, change into sweats, and head off for the gym, or take a jog in the park, or stay home and weight-train. Or you might want to meet friends at the gym, work out, and then have dinner together.

The truth is, there's no wrong time to exercise (well,

maybe not after a four-course meal). Some men enjoy kicking back on weekends, playing a game of pickup basketball or going kayaking or spending Saturday or Sunday morning at the club. Whatever works for you is fine. But you need to schedule some workout time during the week as well. Going all out for two days and then doing nothing (except maybe nursing those bruised limbs) for the other five inevitably leads to sore muscles, midweek lethargy, and the disappointing feeling that this fitness thing isn't working for you; well, no wonder, when you punish your body in an all-or-nothing regime. It's like eating healthfully on the weekends and pigging out for the rest of the week. Three workouts a week: start there and build on your strengths.

GROOMING: A MATTER OF LOGISTICS

Depending on your schedule and where you're coming from (or going to), you'll need to figure out clothes and grooming essentials for the gym. Some guys put on workout clothes, jump in the car or hustle over to the club, work out, and then go home—simple. This section isn't written for them.

But what if you like to get to the gym after work? Then you'll need to pack a bag with your sweats, shoes, and toiletries. You don't want to climb back into a business suit and tie after a long, sweaty session on the Stair-Master. And if you schedule an early-morning workout, it would be great to be able to shower and dress at the gym and leave for work right from there. But for this you need to plan a bit ahead, carrying your work clothes and shaving kit with you.

THE GYM OUTFIT:

- sweats or shorts
- T-shirt or tank top
- socks and shoes
- jockstrap
- gloves for weight lifting
- weight belt for added lumbar (back) support

TO CARRY:

- towels (if the club doesn't supply them)
- shampoo
- soap (liquid or bar)
- razor
- shaving cream or gel
- talcum powder
- deodorant
- comb and brush
- foot powder or liquid (if you have athlete's foot)
- toothbrush, toothpaste, and floss

FOR YOUR "GOOD" CLOTHES:

- A garment bag with separate compartments for shoes, socks, underwear

CHAPTER FOUR

Monitors

HEART RATE—AT REST AND EXERCISE

Technically speaking, your heart rate is the number of times your heart beats in a minute. Monitoring your heart rate will determine how hard you are working and how efficiently the heart works at rest. By testing your heart rate at any given time, you can see for yourself just how well that pump of yours is working.

The most important reason to exercise is to help the heart work with less effort. By stressing the heart in a suitable and safe fashion, you will help the muscle of the heart beat slower, causing a larger volume of blood to flow through your veins, and therefore beat fewer times per minute than it did before you exercised. By doing so, the heart delivers more oxygen to the body and flushes your veins (cleaning out the plumbing).

The best places to check your pulse, or heart rate, are at the carotid artery (to the side of the throat, just under the jaw line), the radial artery (at the wrist, just below the thumb), and the temporal artery (at the temples on either side). Touch the areas lightly and find the beat before you start to count.

This heart rate is determined by counting your heart beat for 10 seconds and then multiplying by 6 (equals 1 minute). Begin at zero.

10-SECOND HEART-RATE CHART

10-SECOND COUNT	BEATS PER MINUTE	10-SECOND COUNT	BEATS PER MINUTE
8	48	22	132
9	54	23	138
10	60	24	144
11	66	25	150
12	72	26	156
13	78	27	162
14	84	28	168
15	90	29	174
16	96	30	180
17	102	31	186
18	108	32	192
19	114	33	198
20	120	34	204
21	126		

Keep track of your heart rate: It will tell you if you are working at a reasonable rate. The percentages below will help you understand the percentage of your output. Many men's fitness guides and magazines refer to the training heart rate and target percentages.

Your target heart rate is the rate at which you train most effectively. The formula to determine your target heart rate is as follows:

BEGINNER–INTERMEDIATE

$220 -$ age $=$ (max heart rate) $\times 60\% =$ low target

INTERMEDIATE–ADVANCED

$220 -$ age $=$ (max heart rate) $\times 85\% =$ high target

EXAMPLE OF 30-YEAR-OLD:

$220 - 30 = 190$ (max heart rate) $\times .60 = 114$ beats
$220 - 30 = 190$ (max heart rate) $\times .85 = 162$ beats

The lower end of the target zone (60% to 70%) is where you should train for good health. If your heart beat is slower than those in your age range, you need to push a bit harder. If your heart is beating much faster than those in your age range, you should consider slowing down.

TARGET HEART RATE (PERCENTAGE OF MAXIMUM)

AGE	60%	70%	75%	80%	85%
under 20	126	147	158	168	179
20	120	140	150	160	170
25	117	137	146	156	166
30	114	133	142	152	162
35	111	130	139	148	157
40	108	126	135	144	153
45	105	123	131	140	149
50	102	119	127	136	145
55	99	116	124	132	140
60	96	112	120	128	136
	BEGINNER		INTERMEDIATE		ADVANCED

TALK TO ME

Your heart rate and the intensity with which the heart muscle is working can be measured in a simple yet effective way just by talking. Sounds too easy, I know, but by talking you can realize how hard you are or aren't working. If you can carry on a conversation easily, you are exercising in the presence of oxygen (aerobically). How hard you are breathing is an indication of how hard you are working. If the conversation becomes difficult, you'll know that the intensity is greater. Thus, working aerobically (with oxygen), the system has changed and so have the demands on your heart and lungs.

I like the talk test because it allows you to monitor yourself without stopping and starting. If you are running with a buddy, it is easy to keep track of how hard you are working when you can't answer a question or respond. I don't want to mislead you; you don't have to deliver a dissertation out there while you are exercising, but

an occasional sentence, a possible sales pitch, a pickup line, a lyric to a song, are easy for you to say out loud. The information you get from how labored the line is can help you boost your energy or tell you to pull back when you are going too hard. Talk to me.

PERCEIVED EXERTION

This mode of monitoring is as reliable as the body itself. Your body and the systems you use while exercising will tell you when you need to rest. If a weight is too heavy, you can't lift it, so don't lift it. It you have lifted enough, your body will tell you to stop. The same with aerobic movement and cardio training. If your body wants to stop because it needs rest, it will.

You have to inhabit your body and listen to what it is telling you. If you touch your tongue to a cold piece of metal, it will stick. If you touch a flame, you will get burned. The same holds true with exercise and weight training. I realize that your body doesn't sustain itself in running motion without your brain telling your feet to step quickly in front of each other repeatedly, but if your body gets tired it will stop.

REST AND RECOVERY

For many men, rest and recovery are translated into lazy and weak, or not being man enough to take the test. The male ego often gets in the way of real progress and can interrupt a smart and effective commitment to attaining realistic goals at all levels.

In the case of training too hard or too fast, recovery periods are important to reduce the chance of overtraining and injury. If you get injured, it's best to see a physician familiar with musculoskeletal health and injuries. Getting a specific diagnosis for your injury is vital to your recovery. Ask your doctor if the injury is a tear or strain in the muscle, a tendon pull, a ligament sprain, or an irritated bursa. Bursas are sacs filled with fluid surrounding joints and muscle tendons; these sacs guide and lubricate the joints and muscles. Inflammation of the bursa is called bursitis. Tendinitis, on the other hand, is inflammation of a muscle tendon. Tendons are positioned on the ends of the muscles, where they attach to the bone. Acute or chronic pain occurs when the tendon is inflamed, most often felt with movement of the muscles or joint.

Don't settle for a generic diagnosis, one that generalizes the problem, which makes many of us feel like we have been robbed of some interesting detail or have been let off the hook and can get back to our training schedule as if nothing ever happened. Ask for specifics, the names of the muscles affected, the bursa or ligament involved in the movement, and the specific treatment for the problem. Asking for information will prove to your doctor that you want to be made aware of the process and it will keep him on his toes. If he doesn't have time for you, find a doctor who will take the time. If the answers confuse you, write down the name of the muscles or part of the anatomy that is in question, as confusing as that might be, so you can get more information later from the Internet or from an encyclopedia at the local library. Knowledge is power, and the power to take charge of your body and to care for it is intoxicating.

If you can't get to a doctor for immediate care the instant an injury happens, remember RICE: rest, ice, compression, and elevation.

Rest. Get off your feet and rest the affected area to avoid making the injury worse than it is.

Ice. Put ice on the area immediately following the injury for at least 10 minutes to decrease pain and swelling. The ice will also force you to stay in one place, ensuring that you rest and get off your feet.

Compression. Apply pressure around the injured area with the ice; use enough compression to stop the swelling or use an elastic wrap later to maintain compression around the injured joint.

Elevate the injured site to drain fluid from this area; this will help reduce the swelling and keep you in one place.

The RICE method is smart advice and is good to know if you choose to get active. When you engage in a fitness program you become an athlete. You train more often than you once did and perform the same exercises athletes do, so why not consider yourself an athlete?

With the new title of athlete comes a positive self-image and the minor aches and pains most athletes live with. Tendinitis and bursitis are the two most common musculoskeletal conditions. Fortunately, depending on the severity, tendinitis and bursitis may heal without any long-lasting effects. Depending on the treatment and with patience, the injury can heal in a period of between two and six weeks. Physical therapy, rehabilitative strengthening, and stretching to restore full range of motion around the joint are very effective and therapeutic. These methods of treatment help alleviate pain, prevent tissue scarring, and restore the injured area to its normal functions.

HOT AND COLD

Hot: When your injury has had an opportunity to heal for a few days, heat is recommended. Heat will increase the blood flow to the localized area, bringing with it healing cells, and it will help relax the muscle tissue. Heating pads, warm washcloths, or microwavable packs should be applied for 10 minutes or so. Make sure the heat is tolerable to the skin. If the heat is too hot, wait for the pack to cool or use a cloth between you and the pack or cloth. It would be advisable to sleep using a heating pad.

Cold: Ice is recommended for an injury for the first 48 to 72 hours, but this of course depends on the injury. Ice will ease the pain by numbing the injured or inflamed area. Ice will also constrict the blood vessels, help reduce swelling, limit the blood flow to the injury, and control muscle spasms. After a minor injury, a sprain or muscle strain, for example, muscles go into a slight state of shock and the body starts to react. Stop what you are doing, sit down or stop moving, elevate the injury, and apply ice as soon as possible. This process will help you realize what just happened and give your mind and body time to

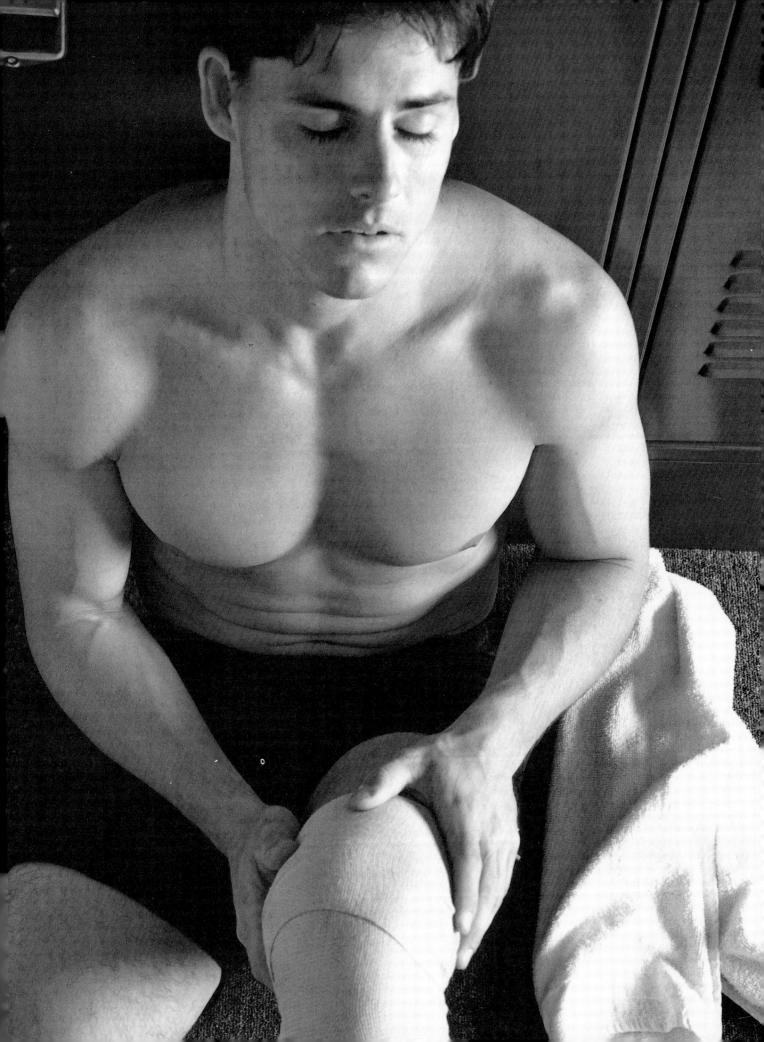

work together while you collect yourself. Ice feels cold and therefore will get your mind off the pain. Apply the ice directly to your skin for about 15 minutes, but if the ice or ice pack is too cold you can put a cloth, a towel, or a shirt in between. Ice will also help those general aches and pains that we have to deal with day to day, but the best way to workout pain free is to train properly and stretch to warm up and finish your sessions. You body will tell you when to stop: and when and if it does, listen!

HALT

Hungry, angry, lonely, tired. This acronym can help you understand why you might be edgy or fly off the handle at any given minute. The sign says it all if you stop and read it. You may seem overwhelmed or exhausted and you have no idea why. The best way to combat these feelings is to halt and ask yourself the following questions:

Am I hungry? When did I last eat something?

Am I angry? Is someone or something making me angry?

Am I lonely? Am I isolated or feeling disconnected?

Am I tired? Am I getting enough sleep or am I overworked?

These simple questions may give you a break and help you out of those same feelings. The answers are quite simple. Eat. Let go. Call someone. Sleep. There is no reason to drag it out or dissect it to death if you don't want to, just halt, think about it and then act on it.

HAVE A DRINK: WATER

Water. Just the mention of it makes me thirsty. It should make you thirsty too. Most of us walk around partially dehydrated most of the time. We really can't get enough water for the amount of activity we do. Even if you haven't started exercising, polls show that our society suffers from thirst.

Three-quarters of the body is water. Don't let this throw the whole fat and lean body weight portion out the window, just realize how vital water is to your wellbeing. If you don't get enough water, it can affect your general health as well as your digestive system.

Many people use water as a dieting tool. The more water you drink, the fuller you seem, thus the less food you will eat = weight loss. It has worked for years, but the real advantage to this scheme is that you are getting the proper amount of water. Sodas and coffee are not the same. In fact, liters of soda and cup after cup of coffee can have the opposite effect, dehydration, besides the impact of the caffeine and the sugar and sodium ingredients.

While exercising you lose a lot of water through sweating, so you should replenish the supply. If your workout program takes off and you find yourself dying of thirst, it is probably because you are. I recommend six to eight 8-ounce glasses of water a day. Research also tells us that water is essential for clear skin. Water adds moisture from the inside, not just from the outside.

PART TWO

Action

CHAPTER 5

Developing a Weight-Training Program

In order to develop a successful weight-training program, you need to understand the three principles basic to success: *intensity* (the degree of overload of the exercise), *duration* (the amount of time of each session), and *frequency* (sessions per week). Generally speaking, the more intense, the longer, and more frequent the program, the greater the benefits. That doesn't give you license to start your workout now and continue until next month without sleep. Use your judgment. Be realistic about these simple principles. Exercise can be like speaking a foreign language: by saturating yourself in the language you can overload. Therefore, duration is like speaking that language for a period of time and the frequency is like taking a language course three nights a week. At that rate you will be speaking fluently in a matter of months, enjoying those benefits and the satisfaction of accomplishment. The same holds true with weight training and its benefits.

To increase strength in muscle, the intensity should be near maximal effort with a low number of repetitions. To gain endurance in muscle, the intensity is lower, but the number of repetitions is higher. So think about it like this. To build size, go heavy. To gain stamina, go light. The size of the weight will dictate to you what area you are in, or at least now you'll have an idea.

Let's try to keep it simple and use 4 to 8 repetitions as the target numbers for strength. If you can successfully lift the weights without losing good posture and technique, you are working correctly. General good health and fitness targets around 8 to 12 repetitions. There is no specific target for the endurance gains, but again work with common sense. For the average person carrying a lighter weight, 12 to 18 repetitions is appropriate for endurance gains.

Strength	**4–8 repetitions**	**heavy weight**
General health	**8–12 repetitions**	**medium weight**
Endurance	**12–18 repetitions**	**light weight**

PRINCIPLES

The following strength-training principles can bring you the success you are looking for. Keep the method simple and focused and you will enjoy all the benefits of your hard work and commitment.

FREE WEIGHTS VERSUS MACHINES

Machines can be used as a learning ground, a smart device to teach you the proper execution of a particular exercise. The only disadvantage is that the rest of the body just sits there and waits for you to finish and move on to the next body part. You will make gains depending on how well rounded your workout is and how rapidly you move from one machine to the next, as well as the weight load you are using. But some men may not have machines available.

By using free weights, you enlist most of the body to assist you in the lifting and lowering of weight with most

as a unit, with each link working collectively to carry the load. Therefore, the same muscles that were described above using free weights would be performed as follows: The quadriceps with free weight would require doing a squat. The squat involves holding the weight and stabilizing the body by contracting the middle of the body; as you perform the squat, the entire lower body (butt, hamstrings, abs, lower back, and the quads) benefits, not just the quads. You are getting more work done in less time.

Give your body and your brain something to do together. Your body will always look for the easiest way to perform (execute) an exercise. Your brain will help the body obtain the maximum benefits by developing your sense of postural balance and building stronger muscles.

PREP WITH REPS

Warming up for a workout is very smart: it puts oxygen into the body, blood into your muscles, and your attention on the period of time you are giving to yourself. Stretching can sometimes exhaust muscles you are going to be using in your workout, so limit the time to five minutes and then perform the exercises you are going to work on with a set of 12 to 15 repetitions with a very light weight. This gets you ready for the heavier load and establishes a range of motion your body will respond to when you get down to business.

exercises. You have to recruit other muscles to help you lift the load for a single muscle group. Open- and closed-chain exercises are what we are talking about here.

Open-chain exercise is just that, an open link of a chain, singular and unattached to the rest of the link system. This is what a machine will offer. You sit on the machine and extend your legs against the weight affecting the quadriceps only, or you sit on another machine and press against the bar that will exhaust only the shoulders. The key here is "only." These muscles are working alone.

Closed-chain exercise closes that link and promotes the chain to work

CHANGE IT UP

It is important for you to develop a consistent approach to fitness and strength, a way to keep interested in working out and enjoying the results. To reduce the boredom factor, you need to change the activities and the program in order to stay interested and to see change. Otherwise, doing the same workout after workout would be like reading the same book over and over again or eating the same meal day after day. The experience becomes ordinary and uninteresting. Even the benefits of the work are reduced because the body has come to expect what it is you are requiring it to do. Therefore, instead of getting on that stationary bike for the five hundredth time, go for a walk or for a swim or even a real bike ride outside. The surprise you set up for your system can re-create a sense of enthusiasm that may be lost in the routine. What it may do is give you a break from the drill.

PROMOTE THE GROWTH

You have to think that strength is a good thing. By getting stronger, you are burning fat from your body and maintaining a healthier machine (body). By not using the machine, you allow the parts to get rusty and its power to diminish. Your muscles will atrophy, getting smaller and weaker. That's the reality.

You want to get stronger. Stronger doesn't necessarily mean bulking up like a fire hydrant. Using your muscles in a safe and effective way will promote the growth and maintenance of strength. This includes the heart and lungs as muscles. By using them you reduce the risk of losing them.

START WITH THE MAJORS AND MOVE TO THE MINORS

Building mass most effectively requires you to work your large muscle groups at the beginning of your workout and then move on to smaller muscle groups. Start with your legs (a major muscle group), move to your shoulders and back (another major muscle group). To push and support the heaviest part of your workout, which in-

volves the major muscles, you need to have the strength to do the job. Then move on to the smaller muscle groups and detailing. If you start with isolation moves, you will exhaust the muscle before it has the chance to work at its fullest potential.

REST

I keep encouraging you by saying, "Get moving!" Well, there is an opposite side of this coin. *Rest!* It is something that your body needs to do in order to recover and repair. When you stress the body and all its systems, it deserves to take a break.

While working out, your body produces lactic acid, which creates that "burning" sensation people say you should go for. When you rest, your blood flows throughout the muscle, flushing the acid along with it. This rest period also allows you to regain your energy and focus for the next set.

Resting between workouts is another type of rest entirely. People get caught up in the everyday workout syndrome, and the by-products of that are negative. Your body requires rest in order to repair. Tearing the muscle while working out stimulates the muscle but your body gets stronger by repairing itself and recuperating. By adding protein to the fiber of the muscles, the muscle grows and heals. It is suggested that you give body parts that you have just trained at least one day off, if not two. It is not advisable to train the same muscle groups two days in a row.

PATIENCE AND ACCEPTANCE

It is important to understand that this process you are undertaking is going to take some time. You will not magically transform into a god overnight, darn it. I wish it were that simple. Many of us are too quick to decide whether or not we really enjoy something, and we are too quick to judge whether or not something that we are doing to improve ourselves is effective and beneficial. Give yourself at least a month or so to decide; if in that time period you haven't seen any results in your body

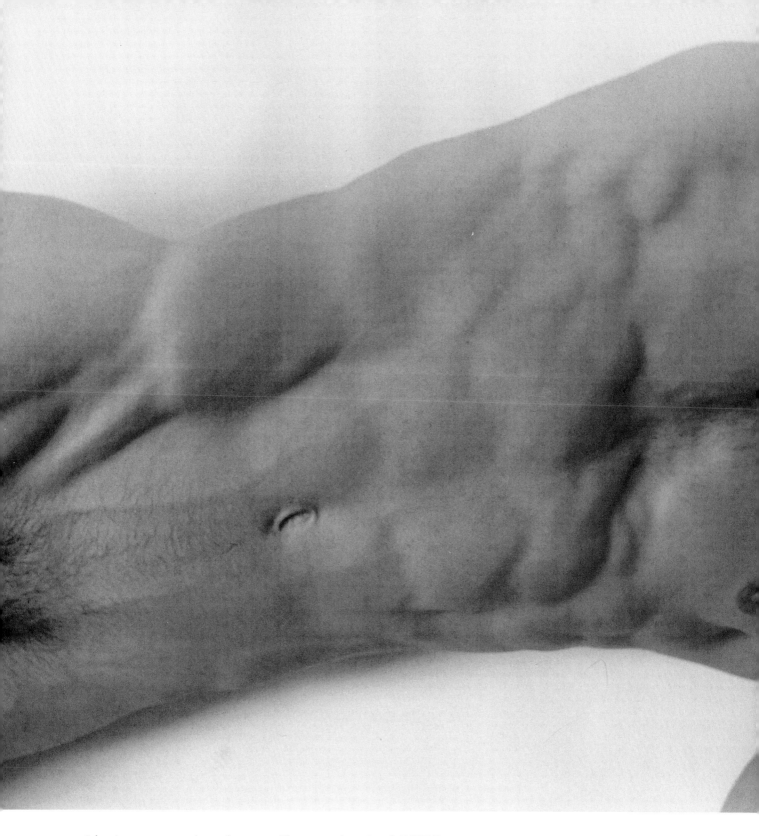

weight, in your strength, or in your self-esteem, then I could see why you would get frustrated and quit. I wouldn't blame you either. But the process will work. "It works if you work it."

SPEED

Take all the time you need and be sure to pay attention to the way you lift and lower the weights. Get into the habit of lifting without using the momentum of your body. Lift and lower the weight slowly. The speed will also change

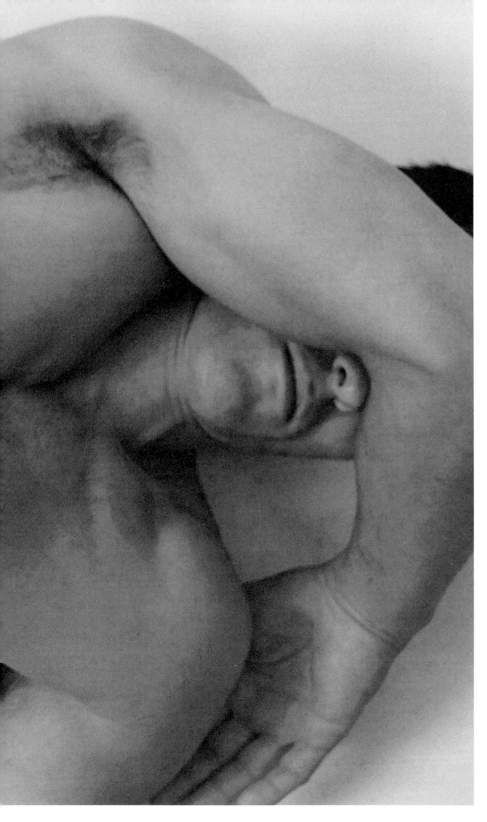

WARM-UP AND COOL-DOWN STRETCHES

Every time you work out you should begin and end with either a few stretches or some type of movement. Many men forget this very essential issue until the damage is done. Start your Basic Training regimen the smart way, and make flexibility as important a component as diet or strength training. The time you spend stretching the muscles that you are recruiting (working) will only help to promote a better performance. Mentally, it will give you time to prepare for the best workout that you can do. And at the end of a workout, the stretch may be a soothing and exhilarating finale, or just a plain old pat on the back. Your muscle system requires a good stretch after shortening and tearing at the tissue, and stretching provides your body with oxygenated blood that will heal and revitalize the body and reduce the stiffness and soreness that comes from training.

WAIT! WEIGHT!

Selecting the appropriate weight is often the problem with many programs. Don't take any suggestions without knowing that you have a choice. Select a weight that allows you to perform the right number of repetitions for the program you have decided on. For general good health and balance, the American College of Sports Medicine recommends

with the size of the weights you are using. Make a conscious effort to lift and lower the weight with technique and precision. The effects will undoubtedly trickle down into all aspects of your training. By staying focused in the present and enjoying the work you have set out to perform, you'll find that the rewards lie within an easily attainable reach.

that you perform three sets of 12 repetitions per muscle group.

Start by lifting a weight you think would be right for you. You can do this in the store if you like, so that you buy the right set of weights. Listen to the salespeople, of course, but most of all listen to your body and hear what it is telling you. If you can lift those weights only six times, and the fifth and sixth were heavy, then leave them there and try another set that is a little lighter. If you can throw those weights across the room, they're too light. Test everything out before you buy it.

Remember, the amount of weight and the number of reps determine what type of training you are performing. Know what you are into and focus on the benefits. It is a good idea to start with a general program for about 8 to 10 weeks. Your muscle systems and cardiorespiratory system will be conditioned and ready for a challenge after that and you'll feel the progress. Then switch your program to either strength or endurance. The variety will be good for you and will offer you new adaptations in the weeks to come.

The number of sets also determines the gains you experience. Even one set of repetitions with the appropriate weight should produce gains for most men. Between three and five sets are recommended for the most gains. That's why you're here, right? To get and see change. Give yourself about one to two minutes of rest. This will give your body enough recovery to perform the next set. Try to stay within that time frame because if you wait too long, your body will cool off and your heart will slow down. You want to remain in a training mode. Longer rest periods waste time and create a longer workout session. Make the most of your time and then get out of there.

Keep in mind that you are working toward a goal and that the rewards have to come from within as well as without. You will see and feel a difference in yourself and that is the true measure of success. Try to enjoy that success: the way *you* feel instead of the way others perceive you.

WHAT'S THE FREQUENCY?

Now that you have an idea of how many sets and reps, the question of how often is the hard pill to swallow. Because we are talking about something you have to do regularly, it can sound a little overwhelming. In beginning a weight-training program, the general rule is to lift weights three times per week. A schedule could be Monday, Wednesday, and Friday or Tuesday, Thursday, and Saturday. This gives you a day off between sessions for rest, and you'll need it. Your body deserves it! You want to concentrate on working each body part (legs, back, chest, shoulders, biceps, triceps, abdominals) with your desired exercises. That doesn't mean you do every exercise in this book three times a week. Take one exercise for each body part and hit it with three sets. This is the best way to set yourself up with a program and to get used to the whole idea of working out. Then move on to the next body part. It seems simple and should be thought of as such.

A split routine means that you do just that, split the work, but that doesn't mean you are doing half the work. In fact, it means the opposite. You perform multiple exercises (more than one) for specific body parts. You also double the number of sessions per week, but you alternate the work. For example, Monday, Wednesday, and Friday you perform chest, back, and shoulder exercises. Tuesday, Thursday, and Saturday you would work legs and arms. This type of training is recommended for intermediate to advanced lifters.

To recap: for the beginning lifter, three times a week, one exercise per muscle group, three sets. When you become more advanced and conditioned you can change your routine into a split routine, six sessions per week, multiple exercises for specific muscle groups. Then it's *your* decision.

PROGRESS

You have to overload you muscles in order to develop strength. You have to force the muscle to contract near

the maximal tension to produce the physiological events necessary for change to occur. Otherwise, the muscle will not increase in size or strength, it will adapt only to the load it is subjected to. Max = maximum gains. Minimal = minimal gains. More effort on your part will produce more of you! But remember, even minimal effort will result in change.

LET THERE BE ORDER

Exercise large muscle groups before you hit the smaller ones. Large muscle groups are legs (quadriceps, hamstrings), back, and chest. The smaller muscle groups assist the big boys; to begin with biceps curls could possibly result in an injury and overstressing the arm. Also, the large muscle groups rely on the support of the smaller muscles, so if you exhaust them to begin the session, you risk compromising the entire session.

Set up your exercises so that you don't continually recruit the same muscles to assist in the next exercise. This offers a bit of rest to the group you just worked to fatigue.

BALANCE

Opposing muscle groups—it sounds like two teams playing in the Super Bowl! Well, if you think about it, it is like that. That back is in competition with the chest. The hamstrings are in competition with the quads. After strengthening one side of the body, you should offer the same work to the other side. This type of thinking and training can create better balance and a great physique. You see it sometimes in men on the street—all shoulders and chest but bird legs. Or legs like tanks and skinny arms. Men will work on the muscles they feel most insecure about and hope the rest will follow along.

The best approach is equal time, balance, and harmony. Your body parts most often work together to perform daily functional movements, so why show a preference to only one side? Think of the body as a whole. This mind-set will create a more flexible, safe, and balanced formula for you to enjoy. Try to remember:

Front of the body / Back of the body
shoulders / latissimus
chest / back
biceps / triceps
quadriceps / hamstrings
abdominals / lower back

THE IDEAL EXERCISES

There are a group of exercises that can be considered the ideal exercises. These are exercises that (when executed correctly) can give you a total workout, hitting every muscle group in the body. They are big exercises that recruit other muscles, from other parts of the body, to assist the targeted group or the area in the body you want the exercise to affect.

Below is a classification of standard exercises that are clearly the backbone of all training programs from Jack LaLanne to Arnold Schwarzenegger to this author. These exercises are so basic that their value can often be overlooked. But in actuality they are effective, proven, and they *really* work. You have seen them before and you will see them again, and there is great reason for that. They provide attention to the major muscles, and when you use the proper weight and perform the proper number of repetitions, these exercises can give you the best workout for your effort.

SQUAT
This exercise can be performed with either a set of dumbbells or a single barbell. Choose your weights for your level, and remember this is a large muscle group that requires a heavier weight in order to overload. This exercise will use all the muscles of the lower body collectively, the quadriceps, hamstrings, and the glutes (butt), of which there are three separate muscles. Your lower back and the abdominal region (core, like the core of an apple)

sitioning the hands wider than the shoulders. Now you are ready to proceed to the foot position.

Position your feet at shoulders' distance apart, not wider than the shoulders, with your toes turned out just slightly. Keep your chest lifted in a natural postural position with your eyes looking directly in front of you and your chin pulled in slightly. As you sit back, shifting your body weight back, the weight of your body and the weight that you are carrying with you should be felt in the legs and buttocks. You want to come down slowly, imagining that there is a chair for you to sit on, but remember there isn't. A 90-degree angle is most effective, but if you modify (make smaller) the exercise while learning it, that is acceptable. Inhale as you bring the weight down and work with a slow and controlled momentum. Lower the dumbbells as if you are putting them on the floor, maintaining your perfect posture. If a barbell is the equipment you are using, your upper body should lean forward slightly using a 45-degree angle. A tip for technique is to keep your elbows positioned under your hands in order to help you keep your chest lifted. When you lower the weight, the tendency is to bend forward; this tip will remind you to sit back and keep the chest lifted. Exhale as you press upward to the start position and feel the heel of your foot pushing the load through the legs. The press-up should stay out of the ball of the foot, to take the stress out of the knee. If you feel pressure

must also participate in order to support the entire exercise. This exercise requires focus, balance, and serious attention to technique in order to be effective. Don't let that scare you; learn it the right way and do it that way every time.

The weight should be held in either hand if you are using dumbbells; hold the weights next to your hips, directly below the shoulder with a relaxed arm. If you are using a barbell, make sure that you get into position when you lift the weight, that you bend your knees and lift with caution. Bring the barbell up with solid form over the head by pressing up using the military-press exercise. The weight should be lowered down behind the head, resting across the trapezius muscle (the meaty part of the shoulder but not on the neck). Your hands hold the barbell with a comfortable grip, po-

also purchase a chin-up rack from a sporting-goods store. This simple piece of equipment isn't as expensive as other types of resistance equipment, and it can offer you a wide assortment of exercises that would add greater variety in the future. The addition to your home gym would have many benefits.

The pull-up will affect the major muscles of the back, including the latissimus dorsi (that wide, meaty part of the back under the arm), rhomboids, which make up the inner part of the mid- to upper back, and the teres major. The closed-chain effect will also recruit the pec and both the biceps and the triceps that make up the upper arms. All of these muscles will work together to pull your weight through gravity. This exercise is difficult. By mastering the pull-up, you will promote that sexy, V-shaped back every man secretly wants. It will also work as a camouflage for the love handles; building the lats makes the waistline looks smaller.

Hold on to the bar above your head with your palms facing away from you. Your should have a wide grip, keeping your hands about eight inches wider than your shoulders. When you extend your body and hang, you will feel the body stretch long, including the arms and abdominals. Breathe in while your muscles are expanded. Pull your body up with control and without swinging your legs. As you get to the top exhale the air and feel the mus-

in the knee, you are not shifting your weight back enough. If you continue to feel the stress in the knee, make the exercise easier by lightening the load (weight), and/or removing the weight completely. Practice by sitting down in a hardwood chair and standing up again repeatedly until you understand the range of motion and the muscles used in the exercise. Just touch your buttocks down on the chair lightly and then stand up again. Keep repeating until you get it

right, then you will be ready to squat using weights.

PULL-UP

This exercise requires a chin-up bar, which is a horizontal bar that is anchored above the head, high enough for you to stretch out the arms completely. Your body can benefit from this standard piece of equipment, so consider one in a doorway, under a deck, or in the basement. You could

cles contract around the abs and under your arms. Hold for a brief pause and then descend slowly, again with control and concentration. You should feel the negative contraction challenge the strength of the back and other muscles that are assisting with the exercise.

DEAD LIFT

Don't look at the name as a negative. The dead lift is an ideal exercise due to the fact that the back, especially the lower back, is such a common area for pain and weakness. This area in the body needs to be strengthened just as other muscles do; however, due to the overuse of the hip and the weakness in the lowest part of the abdominals, the lower back always seems to be dismissed. This muscle group is the opposite muscle group to the abdominals and promotes proper posture and stabilizes the overall body. Not to exercise it is like not finishing a puzzle. Each piece is vital and requires attention.

Along with creating a healthy lower back, the dead lift will strengthen the back of your legs (hamstrings) and buttocks. By supporting the weight in your hands you are also requiring the upper back and shoulders to hold the weight, so there are many overall benefits as well as balance.

Standing with your dumbbells at each side of your feet, or a barbell in front of you, bend your knees and pick up the weight. You should

maintain good posture while lifting. With your feet separated about shoulder distance apart (not wider than the shoulders), your toes turned out just a bit, and your knees bent slightly (soft), you are ready.

Allow the dumbbells or barbell to touch your thighs. Without losing your posture (and I also mean the natural curve in your lower back), lean forward, as if you were taking a bow, until the weight comes in line with your knees. This isn't a contest you are trying to win, so target the knees as the stopping point. You should feel the hamstrings stretching

as you lower the weight. Supporting your midsection with your abdominals, stand back up into your starting position, lifting up through the shoulders, feeling the work in the lower part of the back. The feeling should not be that of pain; if it does feel painful, you might reconsider this exercise or perform it without the use of the weight at all. Avoid locking the knees at all times, with any exercise.

PUSH-UP

The only requirement for this exercise is the ground and good form. The rest is up to you. This exercise lends itself to many disciplines: strength training, self-defense, the military, yoga.

Start on your hands and knees. It is very important for you to position your hands correctly. The hands should be slightly wider than the chest, but at chest level. You can check the position by lying face-down on the floor and positioning your hands next to your pecs, then just adjust them a little wider, so that your hands are directly under your bent elbows. Your hands should be open, palms down, and your fingers positioned with your middle finger pointing forward. By lifting your body off the floor, you just performed a push-up. Depending on your fitness level, you may want to start doing push-ups with your knees bent and resting on the floor. You will then pivot on the knees as you lower and lift the upper body while doing your set of repetitions. Pay attention to the abs so that the body doesn't collapse and sway downward. You can even elevate your buttocks into the air to ensure that the middle of your body doesn't sway. Technique here is crucial, because as you lift up, the chest has to contract and the pectorals have to shorten in order to be effective.

Breathing is also very important to the push-up. As you lower your body, the chest expands and allows more room for air to fill the lungs.

Pressing and executing the contraction requires the muscle to shorten and thus minimizes the space for air in the lungs, therefore you should exhale on the way up. This technique will also help you with momentum and focus. Be cautious about inhaling and exhaling too rigorously, as you may hyperventilate; just breathe normally.

CRUNCH

This exercise requires discipline, hard work, and patience. Many of us want the six-pack you see on all the soap stars and that is the topic of so many television infomercials. The simple truth is that we all have that six-pack (the rectus abdominus), but many of us can't see it due to the layer of fat that is hiding it from the rest of the world. The anatomy of every human being has that same muscle structure connecting the sternum to the pelvis. How you eat ultimately will decide if you choose to show the envied six-pack to the world or not. Some men possess the bulky ab rack that looks like biceps or other strange new muscle groups, but the men on these pages possess attainable midsections. The ideal exercise for the abs is the crunch. This simple exercise will also help prevent lower back pain if performed regularly.

All you need is the floor. Start with your legs elevated in the air with your knees in a 90-degree angle, or by using a chair or bench with your legs on the top to ensure that your lower back is positioned

on the floor correctly. Either position is fine, and always remember that you should work at your appropriate level for any exercise. You should be able to fit your fist under your chin, creating the best position for your neck and for the airflow. If your chin is pinned against your chest, the airflow will be interrupted and limit the range of motion needed for a better contraction. If

your head is tilted back, the cervical spine (back of the neck) is contracted. This position is not recommended.

Start with your hands at your side or resting across your chest. If you have been doing crunches before, to advance, simply bring your hands behind the head and support the head with open fingers, directly behind the ears, holding the head. Try not to interlock or lace up the fingers. This hand position will promote the pulling-up reflex that will happen once your abs start to fatigue. Inhale a comfortable and full breath of air, then exhale slowly, bringing your shoulder blades up off the floor and allowing your hands to slide parallel toward your feet and calves. You will feel the contraction in the front of your body, and by thinking about the ribcage sliding toward your pelvis, in that one contraction you will lock into the proper exercise. Allow yourself to lower your shoulders back to the floor, inhaling as you release the contraction. This movement is very small and controlled, so try not to throw away your technique and just work for speed and repetition.

MILITARY PRESS

There are many exercises that will benefit the strength of the shoulders individually, but none more efficiently than the military press. This classic utilizes all of the muscles that make up the entire shoulder, all three deltoid groups (anterior, medial, and posterior), the traps as well as the triceps in the arms and the upper chest area. As with all the exercises in this section, the abdominals are also included to stabilize of the middle of the body and to ensure proper form. Seated presses sometimes compromise this locked core position, so stand up at attention, holding your gut in and standing tall.

By using a barbell or dumbbells, you can master this very effective exercise. Bending down using your squat position and your lifting technique, hold on to your weight and lift it to a standing position. Keep your feet separated about shoulder distance; if the weight you are using is heavy, split your stance by taking one foot back about four inches or so to prevent swaying while you lift. Bring the weight you're using up to your shoulder level and support the weight by bringing your elbows underneath the hands. The bar should be just under the chin with your hands just outside the shoulder. Inhale evenly and press the weight up into the air as if you were placing something up on a high shelf. The weight should be lifted straight up instead of forward, so be cautious. Lower the weight down to the starting position and repeat to finish your set of repetitions. Keep your eyes looking directly in front of you instead of watching the weight go up and down. The neck should be protected from dropping back because of the pressure put on the upper spine. There was a reference to this contraction in the crunch exercise and it cannot be stressed enough. An unnecessary contraction of that part of the spine will always hamper good form and technique.

These exercises are ideal for everyone to master and perfect. They can offer you a quick workout wherever you are; in a short period of time and with proper execution and consistency you should feel the difference. These simple exercises have been proven over time, and all have the characteristics of a balanced strength-training program. They are, and will always be, the ideals.

TERMINOLOGY

SETS	number of times you complete a full set of repetitions
REPS	number of times you complete a full contraction
CLOSED CHAIN	exercise that requires the use of more than one muscle group
OPEN CHAIN	isolating one muscle to perform an exercise
RESISTANCE	a force that resists another force
AEROBIC	exercising in the presence of oxygen
ANAEROBIC	exercising without the presence of oxygen
OVERLOAD	exhausting the muscle to the point where it cannot perform another repetition
SPLIT	split the body in half (upper and lower) or splitting muscles in the same area (biceps and triceps)
SUPER SET	two exercises performed consecutively for two different muscles without rest
CENTRAL	a neutral postural position, natural spine alignment
CAPACITY	total amount of energy produced

THE BASIC WORKOUT—BEGINNER

Muscle groups, in this order:

BODY PART	EXERCISE	REPETITIONS × SETS
warm-up stretch	jog or march in place 5 minutes	
legs	leg extension	15 × 3
shoulders	military press	12 × 3
chest	incline push-up	12 × 3
back	bent-over row	12 × 3
biceps	bicep curl	12 × 3
triceps	tricep extension	12 × 3
buttocks	standing leg raises	15 × 3
abdominals	crunch	20 × 2
stretches	quad stretch, chest stretch, shoulder-blade stretch	
	hamstring stretch	

Learn these exercises thoroughly to help strengthen the muscles over the entire body with proper technique. Gradually move on to a more advanced exercise level (after approximately six to eight weeks).

THE CIRCUIT

A great technique to reduce the boredom factor. This workout will keep you moving, so expect a sweat. Take the Basic Workout and perform one set of each exercise for each muscle group as listed. After you have completed one set, move to the next without resting and proceed through the entire series of exercises. When you finish one rotation, start from the beginning and repeat three times.

Now you are getting somewhere. Use your knowledge and technique to gain more strength and guide you. Higher repetitions will build your strength endurance capacity. Check your weights and only add or advance when you feel ready. Increase your weight by 2 to 5 pounds, or until the last few repetitions are challenging.

THE BASIC II WORKOUT—INTERMEDIATE

Muscle groups, in this order:

BODY PART	EXERCISE	REPETITIONS × SETS
warm-up stretch	jog or march in place 5 minutes	
legs	squat without weights	12 × 3
	lunges with weight	12 × 3 each leg
shoulders	upright row	12 × 3
	laterals	12 × 3
chest	push-ups	12 × 3
	flyes	12 × 3
back	reverse laterals	12 × 3
	one-arm row	12 × 3 each arm
biceps	isolated bicep curl	12 × 3
	bicep curl	12 × 3
triceps	tricep extension	12 × 3
	tricep dip	12 × 3
buttocks	side lying leg raises with towel	12 × 3 each leg
	supine tilt (one leg up)	12 × 3 each leg
abdominals	crunch	30 × 3 to 4
	crossovers	20 right and left
stretches	quad stretch, chest stretch, shoulder-blade stretch	
	hamstring stretch	

AB-SESSION

If you are ab-sessed, perform all of the abdominal exercises as they are laid out in this book. Rest for 60 seconds between each exercise, and stretch accordingly.

Do the exercises in this order . . .

Crunches	20–30
Crunches with towel	20–30
Reverse curl	20–25
Crossover	20–30 each side
Fish hook	15–20 each side
Back flex	10

THE BASIC SPLIT WORKOUT—ADVANCED

Split the exercises performed into two consecutive days, with the third being a rest day, and then repeat. For example: upper body, Monday; lower body, Tuesday; third day off.

UPPER BODY

BODY PART	EXERCISE	REPETITIONS X SETS
warm-up	jog or march in place 5 minutes	
chest	decline push-up	12 × 3
	flyes	12 × 3
	dumbbell press	12 × 3
back	shrugs	12 × 3
	one-arm row	12 × 3 each arm
	dead lift (light weight)	12 × 3
shoulders	military press	12 × 3
	upright row	12 × 3
	laterals	12 × 3
biceps	isolated bicep curl	12 × 3
	bicep curl	12 × 3
triceps	tricep extension	12 × 3
	tricep dip	12 × 3
abdominals	crunch	30 × 2
	crossovers	20 right and left
	reverse crunch	15 × 2
stretches	quad stretch, chest stretch, shoulder-blade stretch	
	hamstring stretch, half-moon	

LOWER BODY

BODY PART	EXERCISE	REPETITIONS X SETS
quads	squat without weights	12 × 3
	lunges	12 × 3 each leg
	balanced lunge	12 × 3
hamstrings	dead lift (heavy weight)	12 × 3
	hamstring curl with weight	12 × 3
	prone leg raise	12 × 3
buttocks	supine tilt (one leg up)	12 × 3 each leg
	leg raise	12 × 3
	prone leg cross raises	12 × 3 each leg
abdominals	crunch with towel	30 × 2
	crossovers	20 right and left
	reverse crunch	15 × 2
	fishhooks	15 × 2 each side
stretches	inner-thigh stretch, quad stretch, chest stretch,	
	shoulder-blade stretch, hamstring stretch, half-moon	

Your home workouts can be performed three to five times per week. Be sure to provide yourself with enough time to think about technique and about how much effort you are using to get through the workout.

Below, you will see a general rule of how many times to perform each exercise in a given set, and how many sets to perform depending on your fitness level. Nothing is set in stone, so work to the point where you feel good about the work, and then begin to realize and achieve the success you deserve!

KEEP IT SIMPLE

novice / 3 sets × 8–12 reps, light weights

intermediate / 3–4 sets × 10–15 reps, medium weights

advanced / 4–5 sets × 6–10 reps, heavy weights

CROSS TRAINING

Cross training suggests different things to different people, from an activity provided as a break from a regular routine to the highs and lows of spiritual conditioning. Cross training uses alternative training techniques or activities to enhance and improve your performance during your regular fitness program. Think of it as a boost, a shot in the arm, or a way out of the doldrums of habitual fitness training. For example, surfers and skiers often use cycling as a way to maintain the strength in their thighs, increase their aerobic ability during the off-season, and to train for that particular sport. Tennis players use weight training to help them put power into their serves as well as promote the strength in their legs that is required for speed. Cross training will give you an edge and help to decrease overtraining and the burnout factor.

More specifically, cross training offers benefits in these key areas: aerobic endurance, anaerobic endurance, muscular strength, muscular endurance, flexibility, injury prevention, and psychological rest.

DEFINITIONS

• **Aerobic endurance** increases the ability of the cardiorespiratory system to supply oxygen to the muscles that are working. With this type of training you'll deliver more air to the body with less stress.

• **Anaerobic endurance** is short-duration speed training that uses energy to power short bursts of maximal performance without oxygen. For example, sprinting, high jumps, and rowing machines are great activities for improving anaerobic endurance. This type of training tool is very important to the development of stamina in all forms of exercise. It will challenge even the fittest of men.

• **Muscular strength** is the foundation of most physical activities and sports. Your body relies on its strength for explosive, quick movements to carry the load you're lifting. Cross training will overload the muscles by subjecting them to higher stress levels than they are used to. Climbing stairs and lifting weights will overload the muscles and provide strength gains to the same muscle groups that perform other sports or activities.

• **Muscular endurance** means reps. Lots of reps! You require your muscles to contract against a resistance (weight) for an extended period of time. As you get stronger, you are able to perform more repetitions in the same amount of time. Endurance also breeds tolerance in the muscles. As you train this way, your systems can tolerate greater stress loads for a longer period of time.

- **Flexibility:** All the activities you enjoy involve flexibility as a vital component. Yoga and other forms of stretching depend on a wide range of joint movement and promote flexibility in all muscles. A solid stretching program can also reduce the risk of injury, muscle pain, and inflammation associated with stress caused by strenuous exercise.

- **Injury prevention:** Strength gains protect your body against injury, particularly overuse injuries. By cross training, you recruit muscles different from those you use in your usual routine or program. You utilize the muscle with different patterns, allowing more of the muscle to share the training stress. This will help protect vulnerable joints, tendons, and ligaments from damage.

- **Psychological rest:** Cross training with other activities will give you a needed break from your routine. You can still train and reap the benefits of training, but doing something different can liven up your program and motivate you all over again. This type of training technique can also help you break through a plateau and elevate you into a whole new arena of performance and pleasure.

THE FOUR SEASONS

Winter, spring, summer, or fall. Every season has its benefits and downfalls. All you have to do is get your butt off the couch and work! You have to look for the possibilities in every season and enjoy all the aspects each one brings. Don't let the winter darkness and the temperature get you down; get out in the snow or out on the slopes. The season passes quickly, and warm, sunny days *will* return. This is when working out indoors becomes so important, so that you won't lose all the gains you have made and so that when you return to the great outdoors you are ready for anything.

Spring and fall are the seasons that encourage activity and celebration. Everyone feels rejuvenated when spring hits. The temperature and the light invite you out of hibernation and give you the opportunity to get active again. Fall signals the ending of the outdoor season, so people get out and do as much as they can before having to go back indoors. People everywhere should revel in these two seasons and enjoy all the activities they can.

Summer is the hot one; for me it means the beach. Sand and surf, a lake, a river, anywhere there is water, there is activity. Anywhere there is summer, there is activity. This is the season when everyone has more time and more options to get active. Use this opportunity to do just that—join in a game of softball, row a boat, or challenge a friend to a game of tennis. All the hard work you have put in at the gym or at home will pay off by allowing you to perform with some awareness of your body and a level of fitness that might even surprise you. You won't be on the sidelines anymore wishing you could participate; you'll be participating.

HOW OFTEN SHOULD I CHANGE?

Change is a good thing, but once you have found an activity you like, it may be hard for you to find a new one you enjoy just as much. Getting out of your comfort zone and into a new training mode can offer you benefits that you never thought about. That's what cross training is about, changing a habit-forming pattern so that you can excel in the sport of your choice with balance.

Changing your entire routine is difficult. Staying away from an activity after you've become hooked (and I mean hooked in a good way) can be just like taking coffee away from breakfast or brushing your teeth before your shower. It is just a change of habit. You have to be open enough to look at the change as a smart training technique. Switching will allow you to rest your muscles that are most likely working on semiautomatic. A different routine or exercise grouping will give your head something new to think about and establish a new learning curve.

I would recommend that you try to change your sports training every six to eight weeks. After this period of time your body has adapted to the cycle and the muscles know how to respond to the actions you're forcing them to go through. That is also the reason you feel sore after you attempt a new sport. Every activity offers your body something new. Just keep making the offer and your body will respond.

Change with the seasons, change the exercises, change your mind, and see the result!

OPPOSING TEAMS— SYSTEMS

As mentioned previously, balance is essential to a well-rounded fitness program. Cross training exposes you to a variety of exercise methods that challenge the muscle groups you are strengthening in different ways. It's like one team versus the other. Think of it as we discussed earlier: the front of the body versus the back of the body.

Activity 1	/	Activity 2
swimming	/	aerobics
cross-country skiing	/	versa climber
soccer	/	water running
boxing	/	running
cycling	/	golf
tennis	/	jumping rope

Cross training is an alternate technique or action that complements the one you normally participate in so that "your sport" is made better and your performance is at its peak. It is important to note that as you get older, this type of training will also reduce the risk of injury or overtraining. With a variety of exercises and activities, your body requires you to engage in the use of all muscle systems, not just the few that only one sport will use. Pushing your heart and lungs by introducing them to a new method of exercise will keep them healthy and functioning properly. Lubricating joints, distributing oxygen, and increasing the blood flow to all parts of the body are the keys to a healthy body. We all enjoy the by-products of reduced body fat: firm, lean muscle tissue, an efficient cardiovascular system, and the healthy spirit that accompanies all of the above.

CHAPTER SIX

Basic Training: The Fundamentals

EXERCISES À LA CARTE

Choose from among the exercises listed below to tailor your own workout program. Keep in mind that you should train the largest muscle groups first and work your way out to the smaller groups toward the end of your workout. Practice the exercises three times a week, for two weeks. This easy-to-follow method will help you achieve your first goal. Go.

POSTURE AND WEIGHT POSITIONS

CENTRAL POSITION

The central position is a perfect postural position that should be maintained at all times. Ideal spinal alignment offers numerous benefits, not only pertaining to a fitness regimen but also affecting many aspects of your life. The central position is the foundation of safe and effective exercise technique. There is a technique for you to establish the central position, and with practice and awareness it will become second nature to you.

Central position involves the equal contractions of the front and back of the legs in order to support the vital knee joints. It activates the buttocks and hips to support and maintain the pelvis's position and keeps the hips aligned. All of the muscles around your torso contract to support the middle spine and to keep the spine in a neu-

tral, natural position. The chest supports the upper part of the spine and the neck carries the head.

Description: The feet are positioned directly under the shoulders, with the feet turned out slightly (you will read this over and over in the descriptions of the exercises so that you begin to think of the "central" position automatically). Keep the knees bent and your butt tucked under. Try not to exaggerate the tuck; it should feel comfortable. If you tuck too much, you will feel and look odd. Hold the torso firm and support the chest high. Pull your shoulders back as if you had an egg between the blades, and pull your head back just a little, allowing the chin to relax; avoid the turtleneck look (peaking out of the shell). Now you have the central position. In yoga it is called "The Mountain"; in the armed forces it is called "Attention," so you can see that the commonality of this postural checklist is critical.

DUMBBELL POSITION

Hold each dumbbell with a relaxed grip. Try not to squeeze the metal to the point where it would hurt just to hold the weight. Exercise gloves will give you a better grip, and I encourage you to wear them whenever you are lifting. As you drop down to pick up the dumbbells, squat down as you would if you were picking up a delicate package. By doing so, you perform the task with greater attention to the package and your back. Bend both knees and keep your back supported until you grasp the weights, then lift with the legs. This helps you avoid any undue stress to the lower back area as you return to the central position.

Depending on the exercise, you should hold the dumbbells at your side with shoulders relaxed and torso contracted to avoid the arching of your lower back. If the weights are too heavy, your body will also tell you when to put them down.

BARBELL POSITION

The barbell will most always be sitting on the floor in front of you, so use the same technique described for the dumbbells: Bend at the knees with shoulders up; never bend from the waistline to pick anything up.

When holding the barbell on your shoulders behind the neck it is important to understand a few tips that will ensure safety and comfort. Bring the barbell onto the shoulders carefully and rest the weight of the barbell on the meaty part of your upper back, also known as the traps. This will help you avoid resting the barbell on the vertebrae at the upper part of the back and lower part of the neck. You don't want to bruise that part of your body. If you need a cushion, wrap a towel around the barbell and this should feel better. You should try to hold the barbell with a relaxed hand, and your hands can be positioned below the shoulder. This will assist your support of the barbell without causing you to tilt or bend forward when you perform exercises.

HOW TO LIFT

It may seem like the easiest thing in the world, but lifting something off the floor, as you will be lifting weight off the floor, requires a few simple reminders. Size up the load and decide if the weight is too heavy or inappropriate for you to lift alone. Keep the weight close to your feet so that the load won't cause undue stress to your lower back, as it would if you lifted the weight too far from your center of gravity. Bend at the knees and use your arms and legs to lift the load off the floor, keeping your chest up and your back arched forward.

Your back can be as strong as a girder in a building or as fragile as a stick. You should always consider the weight before you lift it. Once your back is injured it is more apt to get injured again. The vertebrae and the disks are a perfectly built piece of architecture, so don't mess around with it. There are many risks, not only with lifting, but lifting is something that you have control over.

The Upper Deck

CHEST

The chest is made up of two muscle groups, the pectorals major and minor. The major, the bigger of the two, spreads across the front of the body from the sternum to the upper arm. This connection also provides the arms with the ability to swing back and forth and assists in the rotation of each arm. The pectorals major are thick and, with the pectorals minor, make up a very strong part of the body, a favorite for men to work. It's the muscle group that most people notice first because it suggests power and vitality. The following exercises provide you with a chest—also known as "pecs"—to be

PUSH-UP (CHEST PRESS)

Come down to the floor for this basic exercise. Begin on your hands and knees, positioning the hands slightly wider than your shoulders. The best way to ensure proper hand position is to come down to the floor as you would if you were sunbathing, lying flat on your stomach. Take your hands to your chest level and then out to the side about three to five inches. Using the chest muscles, press up, extending your arms and lifting your body off the floor. That is one push-up. Your abdominal wall should always be held firm and your hands should be kept open. As you lower your body, you should inhale as the muscles stretch. The theory behind this type of breathing: when the space available for the lungs expands, you should fill the lungs with oxygen. As the muscles around the lungs contract, you should expel the air. This makes a lot of sense and offers you a good supply of air as you work. The force of the exhalation can also give you a boost to the top when you get tired.

Your foot position can also vary depending on how strong you are. If you are just starting out, keep both knees on the floor, using them as a pivot. A towel may be useful, depending on the surface you are on. If you want to advance the level of the difficulty of the push-up, lift your knees off the floor and support the lower half of the body with your feet. Your buttocks should also be positioned slightly higher than they would be if you were lying on the floor. This simple direction will also keep you aware of the abdominal position.

Your head should extend naturally off the shoulder and your eyes should be fixed on the floor beneath you. This will help you focus and stay in the exercise.

INCLINE PUSH-UP

This exercise is similar to the standard push-up regarding focus and technique; however, the position varies. You perform this push-up using a bench or platform in order to stimulate another area of the same muscle group. Variety is the spice of life, and this simple variation can also be useful for beginners to gain strength. If the push-up is too difficult, if the wrist support isn't there, then this exercise is good because is will eliminate 25 to 30 percent of your body weight from the exercise.

If you are flat on the floor, your chest and assisting muscles are pushing and lowering 100 percent of your weight against gravity; by working on the incline you are removing at least a quarter of the weight from the exercise.

Take a bench (piano or weight) and set it in front of you. Bend your knees and place your hands on the bench, with your hands separated shoulder distance. Step both feet back so that your body resembles a plank. Just as it does in the push-up, your midsection stabilizes, keeping

your buttocks in the air. Looking down at the bench and supporting the weight of your body with your chest, lower yourself until you're about an inch away from the bench. Inhale on the way down and then press your body away from the bench, breathing out, with a smooth motion.

This type of push-up will utilize the same muscles as the regular push-up, but the attention will be on the lower part of the chest and the outer edge, the part that creates a well-defined chest.

DECLINE PUSH-UP

The third in the series of push-ups, this version requires more skill than the other two because your feet are above your body from the start. Be careful not to use this exercise if your heart rate is up because it may lead to dizziness. Any time your head is lower than your heart, the blood flow to your head increases. That is one reason people get dizzy when they work out in some positions.

Put yourself in position for a standard push-up, but prop your feet up on a bench. Hands are shoulders' width apart and at chest level. Keep your eyes focused on the floor and lower your body just until or just before your nose touches the floor. You will feel the stretch in the chest as you lower yourself down, breathing in as you go. Exhale as you press up. This push-up hits the highest part of the chest and the definition under the pec.

FLYES

The flyes resemble the wings of a bird, hence the name. This exercise is different from the standard push-up for a variety of reasons. You should perform the flye either on a bench or standing upright, instead of lying on the floor. The exercise requires weights or another form of resistance instead of your body weight. This exercise recruits an alternative contraction for the muscle to perform, and by so doing the muscle reacts differently. Think of the flyes as a sculpting tool, a technique used to sharpen edges and create better definition in the upper body.

Sit down on the bench first and rest your weights on your knees until you are ready to begin. Lower yourself slowly onto the bench with caution, keeping the weights on your knees until you are flat. Bring one dumbbell in by bending the arm at the elbow and holding the weight at the chest and then the other weight to the chest as well. Extend both arms up, lifting the dumbbells over your chest, and keep your elbows soft (bent). With your palms facing each other, you are ready to begin the flyes.

Imagine your arms are wrapped around a barrel; the arms create a rounded position with the weight above. As you lower the dumbbells toward the floor by slowly opening the arms out to the side, feel the pulling of the chest muscles on the outer side of the chest, where the shoulder and the chest interconnect. This is the all-important stretch you need to feel in order to challenge the muscle to get stronger. When you drop the weight lower than your body, stop and press the weight back up to the starting position. Concentrate on feeling the inside part of your chest as you raise and lower the weight against gravity. By doing so you are always present in the exercise and the performance gets a better reaction for the muscles.

If you are using a cable machine (as demonstrated in the photo on page 48) as the weight resistance tool, rely on your posture and balance. Standing between the two points of resistance, take one step forward to promote the stretch in this exercise. Support your upper and lower body by contracting the abs and holding your body steady with a split stance (one foot forward). Hold on to the handles of the cables, which for this purpose should be positioned at shoulder level or higher (many of these resistance machines offer a variation height that you can adjust to your height). Again, with your palms facing forward, squeeze your chest and pull your arms together in front of you with control and precision. Open your arms and feel the stretch through the chest and repeat your set of repetitions. This exercise is a replica of the bench flyes only standing.

SHOULDERS

The shoulders (deltoids) are made up of three separate muscles: the front (anterior), the lateral (medial), and the back (posterior). These work together to move your arms back and forth and lift over the head. Many times men will work the muscle they can see, thus the front of the shoulders seem to be attacked more often than the other two areas of the shoulder. Daily activities and regular functions of the shoulder, such as walking, running, driving, typing, and painting, require the shoulder to contract the anterior deltoid, and then we go to the gym and work that area in the shoulder even more. This will most likely lead to an injury. How can you ask any muscle to do so much when you require so little from the rest of the muscle group? It is as if the anterior shoulder is the Michael Jordan of the shoulder joint and scores three times more than any other player. Your shoulders, however, are not a basketball team, and the "team" should work together as well as the Bulls. Pay attention to all the players of this body part and enjoy strong, well-defined shoulders.

MILITARY PRESS

With a dumbbell in each hand, or a single barbell, the exercise will concentrate on the front, side, and back of your shoulders. This exercise is wonderful because it takes care of three muscles at once. The technique will be the same for both types of equipment, but by using the individual hand weights you must think about where they are in space. It determines unilateral (one: barbell) and bilateral (two: dumbbells) technical skills and the awareness of both types of movement.

Support the weight at shoulder height with a grip that is slightly wider than the shoulders. Your feet should be stabilized, with one foot back about 12 inches to ensure that you don't waiver or sway back and forth during the exercise. Keep your gut tight and avoid arching your back when you have the weight above your head, or at any other time, for that matter. Maintain a neutral grip of the hands, meaning hand over wrist, wrist over elbow, to prevent stress on the wrist and ensure better form. The same will hold true for both types of equipment.

Press the weight up into the air, exhaling as you do, with a smooth and deliberate contraction. Avoid pushing the weight forward and then up; the stress of that action could be dangerous. Hold the weight above the head for a short stop and then lower the weight with a deliberate, controlled contraction. Repeat the set number of reps, and the number of sets (see the Ideals section in Chapter 5).

FRONT RAISE

This exercise targets the anterior (front) shoulder. As with the military press, body position and foot placement are key elements for the best result and execution of this or any exercise. Hold your abs firm and feel the support for the spine, especially the lower part of the spine. Your foot stance remains split or separated about shoulder distance. The split stance secures your body against any front-to-back movement as you begin to fatigue.

Use of a barbell or dumbbells is optional with the front raise: The front raise with dumbbells will be performed with the arms independent of one another; the barbell can only offer both arms working together at the same time.

To prepare for the task, focus directly ahead of you at a spot on the wall and inhale. If using dumbbells, keep your thumbs pointing forward as your arms are resting at your side. Exhale as you lift each dumbbell separately. Lift one hand in front of you, carrying the weight to about shoulder level directly in front of you, no higher. You are working against gravity, so don't expect this to be easy. Lower the weight slowly and then switch to the other side. Try not to race; you have to give time to the process and execute it perfectly every time.

As a variation of the single barbell front raise, the duo raise lifts both the dumbbells at the same time. Pay attention to the way the dumbbells move through space and make sure you have control over them.

The barbell version of the same exercise stabilizes the hand position for you, however, the hands rotate so that the palms face down, rotating the shoulder internally. This rotation has downfalls due to overuse and continued internally rotated exercises that are performed by everyone in daily tasks. By externally rotating the shoulder with the dumbbell you have opened the shoulder and have relieved the pinning of the front shoulder that happens all too often. If you are just beginning a weight-training program, any of these exercises targeting the front shoulder are fine and you should continue with the appropriate weight and sets. Keep it up!

LATERAL RAISE

The lateral raise will broaden your shoulders and give you that swimmer's build that so many men secretly desire. The medial deltoid is the cap of the shoulder and this muscle part may require you to lower the weight that you might be using for the other exercises that we have been discussing. That doesn't mean you should lower the amount of weight so much that you can't feel anything. Nor should you lift such a heavy load that your technique suffers. Monitor yourself and be honest; there is strength behind the form.

Now that the weight load is staying below the shoulders, it is okay to stand with your feet apart, separated shoulder distance, with a contracted midsection. Are you finding this to be a common theme with all of these exercises? Your chest should stay lifted and your arms are extended with a 45-degree bend at the elbow. Holding onto your dumbbells with your palms facing your body (inward), pointing your thumbs in front of you, focus straight ahead and begin by lifting your weights outward with a slow and controlled lift. Lift the weight to about shoulder height and then stop and hold for a moment while your arms are parallel to the floor. Using the exhalation to assist the lift will help to ensure that you aren't throwing your body weight into the exercise. Lower the weight slowly and feel the outside of the shoulder as you ease it down. Repeat the contraction as many repetitions as desired and then rest.

UPRIGHT ROW

Many of the exercises described in this chapter have the option of barbell or dumbbell interpretation. You can use one or the other or both, depending on your home gym budget. With the upright row you can use either/or, the technique would be the same.

Standing tall with your feet separated, knees unlocked and the control of the muscles around your spine, hold your weights down at your side with your palms facing back and your thumbs facing in. The action begins first with the elbows bending and lifting up to the sky, allowing the hands to carry the weight up to about the middle chest region. Breathe out as you lift up and stabilize your movement. Keep the elbows up above the shoulders for a moment and then let the weight descend slowly to the beginning position. Think of this movement as rowing with oars; the range of motion is at a different angle, but the movement is very similar.

If you have dumbbells, keep them separated but directly in front of each thigh. A barbell should be held with both hands separated about hip distance, or position your hands so that your thumbs touch your thighs when at rest.

When raising and lowering the weight, allow the weight to glide near the body and use precise technique at all times. This position should be applied to both the barbell and the dumbbells.

BACK

I have witnessed over the many years of training clients and observing men working out in health clubs and gyms that the attention to the development of the back is overlooked, put on the back burner, so to speak. Wondering why and looking at my own pro-gram, I realized that the back is not visible while working out if you are looking in a mirror. We pay more at-tention to the muscles that we can see, so therefore the back is dis-counted and trained less. The thought of people watching as you walk away should remind you that your back is visible, and to me the back muscle structure is the most incredible and important.

The back is made up of an intri-cate pattern of muscles, the largest being the latissimus dorsi (lats), the meaty side panel of the back, just un-der the arm; the rhomboids, which cover the shoulder blades; and the all-important erector spinae, the part of the lower back that requires special attention. The trapezius (traps), the muscles of the neck that extend into the back, are considered part of the shoulder group, so look for those ex-ercises in this chapter. There is noth-ing sexier nor more commanding than the sight of a well-developed back. Development of this vital body part will promote better posture and equal balance to the overexercise we give to the front of our bodies, namely the ones we can see.

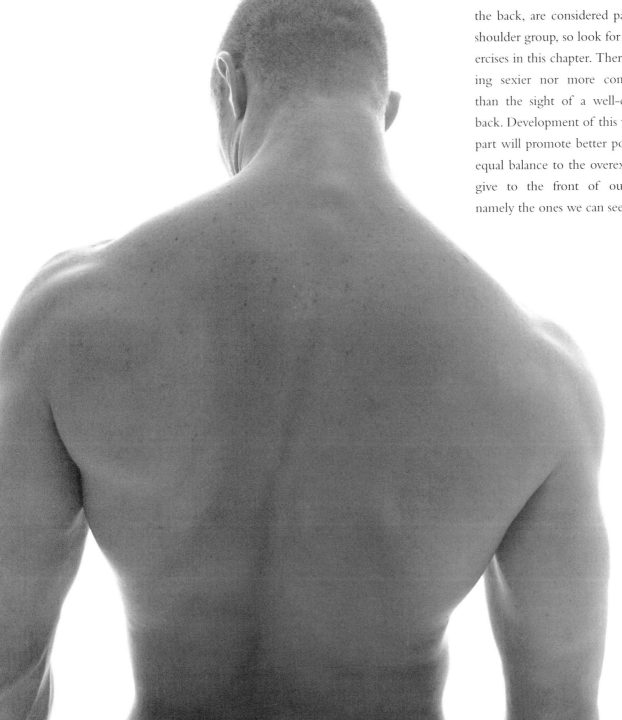

ONE-ARM ROW

This exercise will require you to use a bench for support so that you can properly distribute your weight evenly with attention to maintaining spinal alignment and firm support of the torso. Begin by resting the weight you are using on the floor beside the bench; that way you can assume the correct body position before you begin the exercise. Stand beside the bench so that the bench is perpendicular to your side. Place the knee closest to the bench on top of the surface and bend forward to rest your hands as well. When you bring your upper body down, remember to hold your abs tight to keep your back in the right position. Reach down and hold on to the weight on the floor with a solid grip and lift it off the floor, keeping your arm extended. Begin the exercise by pulling your elbow upward, allowing your arm to glide close to the body, squeezing the muscles of the back and the rear shoulder. Muscles work in combination with each other when lifting and lowering a load, so be aware that you may feel this also on the shoulder. Lift the weight until the dumbbell is next to the hip and the elbow is above the lower back. Pay specific attention to the torso and maintain a parallel position so that the body

doesn't start to twist or thrust in order to get the weight up into the air, and keep your eyes on the bench to promote a steady body placement. Hold at the top and slowly release the weight back to the starting position; repeat until you have finished the required amount of reps for the set.

When you are finished, put the weight down and turn your body around to perform the same exercise on the other side of the back. Remember the head position is very important in keeping the focus on the exercise. This type of training awareness will keep the contractions in the muscle by the suggestion of the brain instead of the visual reliance we so often require to get through the work.

BENT-OVER ROW

This exercise is very similar to the previous exercise, but here you are using two hands at the same time. Both a barbell or hand weights will give you a very effective back exercise. Keep both feet on the floor, about hips' distance apart. Support the middle of your body in a half squat (your buttocks back) with the weight held in front of you with your arms extended. Pull both elbows back-ward, keeping the weight lower toward your navel. You want to squeeze your shoulder blades together to get the proper contraction. Move slowly through space and then return to your beginning position. You should feel this exercise in the middle part of your back; it will help produce a thick upper body.

REVERSE LATERALS

Set up your station by putting your weights in front of
the bench. You should consider using the same weight
you use for the lateral raises for the shoulders. This
weight would be appropriate in the beginning; as you get
stronger, think about lifting heavier weight, but advance
the weight by small increments.

Sit down on the bench with your feet directly in
front of you. Lean forward and grab your weights from
the floor. Stay down with your upper body over your
thighs, focusing your eyes on the floor in front of you.
Lift the weights out to the side, away from the middle of
the body, with your arms bent at 45 degrees. Think
about the muscles contracting between the shoulder
blades as you lift the weights with a smooth, elevated lift,
maintaining the body position without lifting, and a controlled release to the bottom. The exhalation comes
when you are lifting, the inhalation as you relax. At the
bottom of the contraction try not to allow the weights to
swing; rather, control them at all times. This will cause
the muscles to think as they work.

SHRUGS

The shrug is very similar to the movement you used as a kid, when asked by any authority what you were thinking, and your response was "I dunno." If you think of that expression and the way that body moved, if you can think that far back, you most likely shrugged your shoulders. Well, who knew that you would once again, and again and again, do that same "I dunno" to build the strength of your back and shoulders.

Stand with the dumbbells or barbell in your hands, the weight resting in front of you with your arms fully extended. Place your hands so that the palms are facing back, separated about hips' distance apart. Your shoulders are in a comfortable, relaxed position and your posture is in neutral. If you have been reading each description thoroughly, you will always read about the torso or core stabilizers. You should always remind yourself of that point.

Keeping your arms extended, lift only the shoulder up toward the ears as high as you can go without bending the elbows to assist. The lift is in the trapezius, the meaty part of the upper back that slopes off the neck to the shoulders. Feel the weight in the upper part of the back as you rotate the shoulders back slowly and squeeze the shoulder blades together as you did in the reverse lateral raise. This action will also promote healthy rotations of the shoulder joint at the same time it builds strength in the upper back muscles. The weight may need to be heavier with this exercise due to the fact that this body part is rather strong with all the daily tasks it performs, so to build strength and size you may have to add weight.

A variation you might like would involve positioning the weight behind you. That would mean you would hold the barbell behind you with the same hand grip, or if you are using dumbbells you would have to think about the position of the single weights. Lift the shoulders as you would if you were using the barbell and then lower them down again. Use a precise and controlled lift, holding your body tall and your eyes focused. Repeat as much as you need to complete your goal and then continue with additional sets.

DEAD LIFT (NOT ILLUSTRATED)

The dead lift is an important exercise and should be considered as vital as the crunch is to the abdominals. The erector spinae creates a balance that will prevent back pain; it works like armor around the lower lumbar and the vertebrae of the lower part of the spine. These muscles support the flexion and the extension at the center of the body, where the risk of injury is fairly common. If you suffer from constant lower back pain, consult your doctor for specific exercises you should stay away from or exercises that address your specific problem.

Stand with your feet separated at shoulders' distance with your toes turned out slightly. Your weights (dumbbells or barbell) should be held at the side of the thighs with your hands about hips' distance apart and your palms facing back. Stand with neutral posture and your knees soft (bent a little). Start by bending at the hip, letting your upper body bow forward, keeping your weights and hands close to the legs, bringing the weight down to the knees or just below the kneecaps. Control the forward bend and try not to let the weight go past the joint of the knee to ensure your form and allow the lower back to gain strength. You should also feel a stretch and contraction of the hamstrings. This exercise will provide you with overall benefits. As you lift the upper body back to the starting position, squeeze your buttocks and thighs, maintain the natural arch in your lower back, and come back to a standing position, no more no less. When you arrive back into your neutral posture, squeeze your shoulder blades together a little to add an element to the upper back as well. Due to the fact that your upper back is also supporting the weight in your hands, this exercise requires attention and good form. Your back will thank you.

ARMS

Bis and tris, "the guns," no matter what you call them, they are the calling card to looking fit. If you see a man with a well-developed upper arm, you may automatically think that he is in shape. It is one of the cosmetic physical tricks that creates an illusion of a fit man, unless your commitment is beyond the aesthetics. The arms are divided into two sides, the front (biceps) and the back (tri-ceps). The biceps are made up of two (bi) muscles and the triceps are made up of three (tri). That would indicate that the triceps actually make up more mass in the upper arm than the biceps, therefore requiring more work. Don't concentrate only on the muscles you can see; re-member, there is a whole world out there looking at you from behind.

BICEP CURLS

A classic exercise that concentrates on the front of the arm. Hold a dumbbell in each hand with your palms facing your thighs. Stand with your feet apart, about shoulders' width, keeping your knees bent. Try to contain the movement of the body as you lift and lower the dumbbells from their start and finish positions. Bend one arm at a time, rotating the palm to face the front shoulder. Bring the weight up to shoulder level with a slow lift and a short pause at the top of the contraction. Lower the weight to the hip and repeat on the other side. Alternate each arm until you have completed a full set of single repetitions of the set number for each arm independently, not collectively.

If you are using a barbell, all the positions stay the same; however, the hands cannot rotate because of the single bar. Therefore, keep your hands with your palms facing forward and commence with the exercise as described. All of the same techniques apply.

ISOLATED CURL

This type of isolation does not mean you have to sit in a dark room and work your arms; it means that the muscle will be challenged on its own, without the assistance of any other part of the body, except the brain.

Sit down on the bench and spread your feet apart fairly wide. Bring your upper body forward by bending at the waist. Take one hand down and grab a dumbbell off the floor in front of you and rest the free hand on your thigh. With the arm that is supporting the hand weight, stabilize the elbow against the inner thigh on the same side of the body and hold it there. Don't let it move or slide around, keep it touching the thigh at all times during this exercise. Bend the elbow and bring the weight up to the shoulder and squeeze the bicep tight. Hold for a second and then lower the weight. After a few reps you will feel how difficult this isolated curl really is. Repeat until you reach your set and then move to the other arm.

TRICEP DIP

The triceps are considered (by this author) to be the sexiest muscles of the body. The three muscles that make up the triceps are often recruited to perform so many other tasks. It seems as though they do more than their share of work. But when you need to work them, you need to work them hard. An ideal way to give your triceps the challenge and overload they need is by using your own body as the weight they need to fatigue. This is one of those exercises you can do anywhere, from the privacy of your home to the ledge at the park. Any exercise that requires you to support your own body weight is perfect for travel, and this is one of them.

Sit on the bench you have available with your hands resting at your side. Take your hands beside your hips and place them palms down on the bench. Your fingers should come off the edge of the bench and wrap around comfortably, to stabilize the hands from slipping. Lift your weight off the bench with your arm and shoulder strength and contract your abs for a central position. Shift your weight forward from the hips, away from the bench about two inches or so. No more than that; you do not want this to go to your shoulders. With your feet flat on the floor in front of you slowly bend your elbows, low-

ering your erect torso downward toward the floor. You should resemble an elevator going down and up an elevator shaft rather than down and up an escalator (diagonally). Isolate the triceps by maintaining your elbows directly behind you, not bowed out to the side. As you lower your weight down, think of scratching an itch at the lower part of your back. It's okay if you skim the bench in order to understand what I mean.

Focus in front of you as you press up through the back of the arms, and as you reach the top, press your shoulders away from your ears to complete the contraction. Hold the shoulders down away from your ears at all times, not in a shrug position, which is most commonly the problem in this exercise. Repeat your set number of reps and continue.

TRICEP EXTENSIONS (BENCH OR STANDING)

This exercise requires astute awareness of your body, the center of your universe. Using the bench is the best way to learn the exercise ahead, and then you graduate to a standing position. I want you to understand the importance of the form and then move on to the gains.

Position your weight on the floor next to a bench or platform. Rest your knee on the bench first and then lower your upper body down to the bench, resting your hand on top. Reach your free hand down and grasp the weight off the floor. Now you are ready. Bring your arm up alongside your torso, pressing your upper arm against your side with your elbow slightly higher than the body itself, with the dumbbell in hand. Press the weight by extending your arm fully, carrying the weight behind you until you feel the back of your arm flex completely. Hold on for a moment and then slowly release down to the start position. Maintain a firm torso, shoulders parallel to the floor. Anchor your shoulders as you lift and lower the weight during this exercise. It could be dangerous to throw your body into the momentum. If this is happening, you should consider decreasing the weight of your dumbbell. Repeat until you have finished your reps and sets.

Training note: Changes in the range of motion and the rhythm of raising and lowering the weight you are holding (instead of the constant up-and-down rhythm that seems automatic) can cause the muscle to react more intensely than with a standard curl. Use this technique to shake up your routine and confuse the muscle. Don't let your muscles get into a rut. Doing the same thing over and over without variation can get boring and monotonous. Offering a different tempo or length of stretch to any muscle will cause the tissue to react in a way that it hasn't before. Try to bring the weight up in one count and down in three counts, or up in two and down in two. Your mind makes the suggestion to the muscle, but the brain is not doing the work.

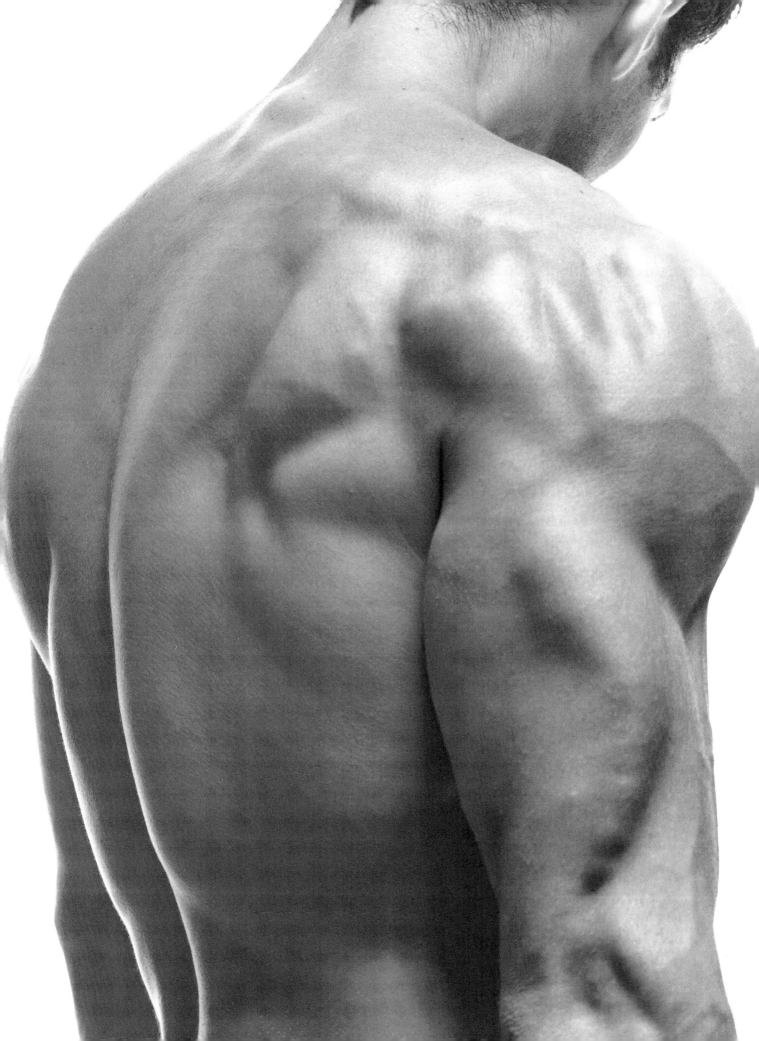

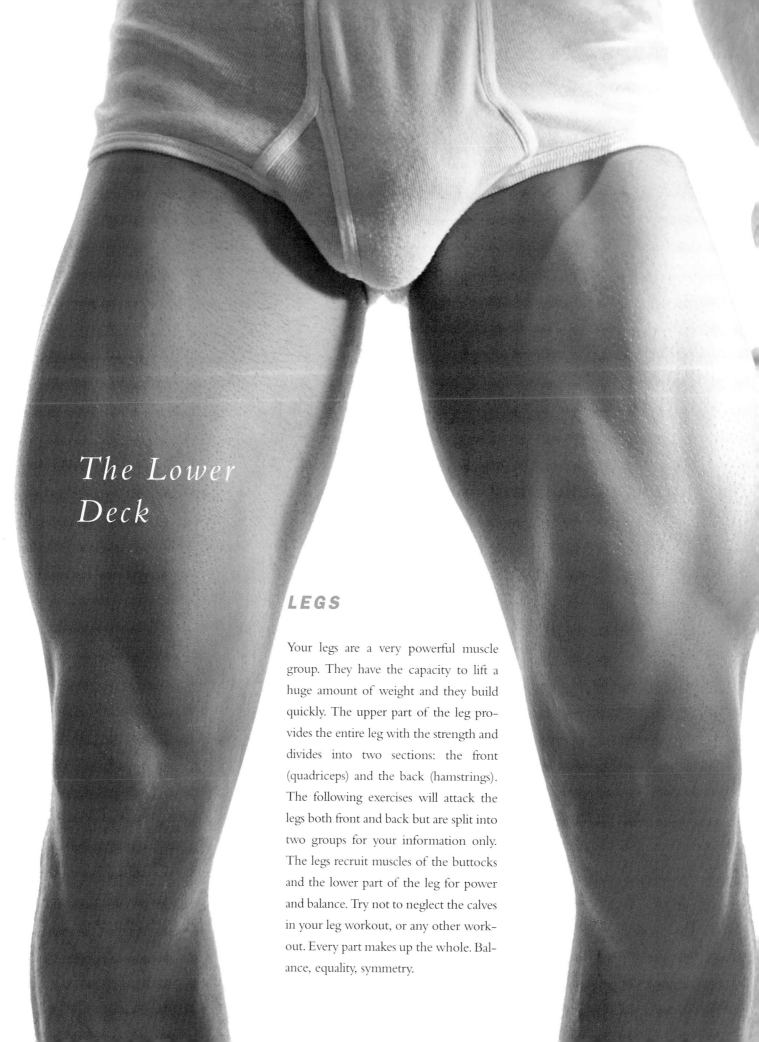

The Lower Deck

LEGS

Your legs are a very powerful muscle group. They have the capacity to lift a huge amount of weight and they build quickly. The upper part of the leg provides the entire leg with the strength and divides into two sections: the front (quadriceps) and the back (hamstrings). The following exercises will attack the legs both front and back but are split into two groups for your information only. The legs recruit muscles of the buttocks and the lower part of the leg for power and balance. Try not to neglect the calves in your leg workout, or any other workout. Every part makes up the whole. Balance, equality, symmetry.

QUADRICEPS (FRONT THIGH)

LUNGES

Keeping this exercise stationary is important. You may have seen a similar exercise where you step forward and press yourself back to the starting position, which is indeed a great exercise, but I have decided to stabilize it to ensure a safer, more precise exercise, one that targets the quadriceps as well as the assisting muscle groups. The position will keep both legs working in unison and will offer you more exercise in less time.

Hold your dumbbells in each hand. If using a barbell, rest the barbell on your shoulders, back far enough to rest on the traps, the fleshy part of the upper back, keeping your elbows under your hand and your central posture position intact.

With your feet separated a little wider than your hips, slide one foot directly back behind you, similar to the yoga lunge stretch; but remember, this is not a stretch, so try not to step back too far. Keep your front knee directly over the foot supporting the leg and balance with the weights at your side or the barbell on your shoulders. This is where technique and attention play an integral part in your success. Hold your upper body so that your shoulders are in line with your hips, which are in line with the knee below you. The knee below you is connected to the foot behind you. It is important that you understand that your body weight should be distributed into both legs. If your body weight is uneven you will feel it immediately.

Lower yourself into the leg positioned behind you, slowly and gradually, until your knee is three to five inches from the floor. Use the elevator visualization that I described earlier, going up and down vertically. This will secure your torso and prevent you from leaning forward. Focus your eyes ahead and think about your balance. When you reach the low end of the contraction (the stretch), squeeze the thighs and buttocks, lifting your body upward (the flex) to your starting position. Breathe evenly here at all times and keep the attention on both legs and your upper body position. Repeat until you have completed the set number of repetitions and then move on to the next set on the other leg. The same rules apply. Finish the set on the other leg and then rest for a moment before you repeat with the first leg . . . and so on.

EXTENSIONS

This exercise does not require weights to be effective, but the use of a strap-on ankle weight would advance the level of the exercise once you have gained the knowledge and the technique required. Sitting on the bench is the best place to start, and then gradually you can take this to the floor to advance and then add weight. This type of progression would happen over the course of a few months rather than just a few sessions.

Sit on the edge of the bench with your legs extended in front of you. Bend only one leg and take hold of that leg with both hands. Lift up through the torso and chest and pull your shoulders back. Now that your posture has been secured, you are ready to lift the extended leg up. Flex the foot, pulling the toes toward you, and elevate the fully extended leg up to the point where it will touch the arm holding your bent knee. You will need to pull in your stomach to help, which means your abs are giving you some help here. You will feel the top surface of your thigh tense and shorten as your leg lifts up. The tension is very specific; you know when you are doing this right. Then lower your leg back down toward the floor, but stop just before you touch. Repeat until your set is done and then switch to the other leg. An alternative position that will target the inner thigh muscles would be the same exercise with a minor rotation of the entire leg, including the foot, out to about a 45-degree turn. Then perform the exercise as you did before and feel the difference.

SQUATS

A perfect exercise when done correctly, the squat affects the entire lower body like no other exercise. There are many positions and variations for the squat, with or without weight, on a machine or even with your legs at different height levels. The most important thing to think about with regard to the squat is execution. Form is important in every exercise, but the technique involved with this exercise will safeguard against the risk of undue stress to the lower back and knees. Pay attention to the directions and look at the demonstrations carefully.

Using dumbbells will be very similar to the everyday action of lifting something off the floor. You can learn the exercise by sitting down on your bench and standing up again. You will use all the same muscles and the same formula to perform the squat without the bench. Hold the weights in both hands with an easy grip. Your feet should be shoulder distance apart, not wider than your shoulders, with your toes turned out a bit. Now shift your body weight back on to your heels and sit as you would if you were going to sit on the bench again. But as you get to the bottom, about a 90-degree bend, stop and hold for a second before you stand up. Then press through the entire leg, including the buttocks muscles, and stand up completely. That is it—clear and simple.

If you begin to feel any stress in your knees, you have to pay attention and keep your knees positioned over your feet. Always maintain a tight torso and focus your eyes on a spot on the wall ahead of you. Looking up or down will ultimately result in a technical error. The use of a barbell would require you to hold the barbell in front of you or on your shoulders. Learn the exercise first and then proceed to the next level.

BALANCED LUNGE

The lunge is a highly effective exercise on its own, but the balanced lunge adds new meaning to the term "leg-work." This exercise is a personal favorite of mine and is challenging and effective. Start by standing about three feet away from your bench or chair. It is very important that you have a wide stance in order to get the full effectiveness of the exercise. Holding the weights in your hands at your side, extend one leg back until it is just under the bench. Then lift the foot up and rest the toes on the top of the bench. This is a balance position, so if you need to practice without the weights, do so until you feel comfortable with the range of motion.

Begin by slowly bending the knee of the leg supported behind you by the bench. Make sure that the floor-supported leg (the front leg) maintains a stable position, with the knee directly over the front foot. The knee position is vital for the exercise to benefit both legs: (a) so it will overload and fatigue the leg on the bench and (b) so it will protect the floor-supported knee from hyperflexion.

Contract the front of the leg on the bench as you raise yourself up, and squeeze the buttocks as well. You will feel this exercise immediately, so be brave and get through your set. Repeat the same on the other leg and feel the benefits in the morning.

HAMSTRINGS (BACK THIGH)

HAMSTRING CURL

All you need for this exercise is the floor, and the one you're standing on will do. Get down on your hands and knees as you would if you were going to do a push-up. Keep you shoulders relaxed and your arms steady, with unlocked elbows and open hands. This body position is going to challenge your central position because the spine should stay in perfect postural alignment; however, the plane is horizontal instead of vertical, meaning your body is parallel to the floor, not erect. Hold that crawling position and work one leg at a time. Try not to allow the middle of your body to sway downward, and keep your eyes on the floor.

Your working leg will bend in the shape of an L. You will feel your buttocks contract in order to support the leg off the floor. Your thigh should be even with the floor, your calf and foot pointing up. Simply extend the leg, keeping it parallel to the floor, and then bend it again. You will feel the hamstring pull and get shorter as you pull

your foot in, and the stretch should be felt as you extend the leg. Work with even contractions and momentum. Don't race through this exercise. Your hamstring works just like the bicep on your arm. It will shorten just like your arm muscle, so if you use that image of the muscle working in the same way, you can see, in your mind's eye anyway, the hamstring working. Inhabit your body.

On the bench you will lie flat on your stomach, but to get there is a bit odd. You have to stand at the end of your bench with a single dumbbell between your feet. Bring your knees to the end of the bench and touch the bench with your knees. Take your hands down to the bench and slowly bend the knee, with the weight between your feet so that you are on your hands and knees on the bench. Now lay flat on your stomach without dropping the weight. I never said this one would be easy. This is the most difficult to set up, but it has great benefits.

Now pull the weight with slow control until you feel your hamstrings contract as described above. Be cautious about the weight and release it back to the original position. If you are having a difficult time you can lie on the floor also. Repeat to complete your sets.

DEAD LIFT

This exercise requires either the dumbbells or barbell and the all-important central position. The dead lift is a classic and will promote a healthy back and help with the flexibility of the hamstrings. We discussed how this exercise benefits the back and shoulders in the Ideals section on page 57, so for now we will pay attention to the benefits for the hamstrings. By bending from the hips, this exercise causes the hamstrings to stretch and contract as they would in daily life. We bend like this all the time, so by strengthening the "hams" you increase the ease with which you live.

Holding dumbbells or the barbell requires the same form: Find your central position and hold the stance for a second. Bend your knees just a bit (soft) and slowly bend forward as if taking a bow after a fantastic performance. Keep your back in its natural alignment and bend forward. Keep your hands close to your legs; in fact, as you learn, let your hand skim your thighs until you reach

the knee landmark and then raise your upper body back to the beginning position. Slowly bend forward again and feel the back of the leg stretch; as you begin to lift, feel the uppermost part of the leg and squeeze your buttocks to assist the lift to the start point. Pay strict attention to this exercise and work within the boundaries I have set for you until you gain the strength in your lower back. With time and consistency, you can lower the weight past your knees, but only by a limited amount. This will ensure the best improvement without undue risk.

The lower part of the leg is often abused and forgotten. This small muscle group (the gastronemius and soleus) is asked to perform great tasks, as you roll up on the balls of your feet, spring your foot with each step you take while walking, running, or jumping rope, and make quick directional changes in the heat of a great set of tennis, even the simple task of pointing your toe.

These two muscles require more repetitions than other muscles because they are accustomed to the regular amount of work they perform in everyday activities.

CALF RAISES

Use your body as the weight to perform this exercise. You can use both feet at once or, if you prefer, one at a time. This exercise does require some balance, so if you need the support of a chair or wall, grab on and let's go. To maximize the exercise stand on a board or step at the ball of your feet to stretch the calf.

Stand in your central position with both feet flat on the floor. Lift up on the balls of the feet and feel the back of your calves tighten like tennis balls. Focus your inner eye on seeing this exercise and feel the work without looking down. Lift with a slow and controlled motion and then release back down to the floor.

You can choose to perform the same exercise using one foot at a time by holding one foot behind the other, resting the foot on the working ankle. Repeat on the other side and finish your required reps. Stretch with the calf stretch on page 130.

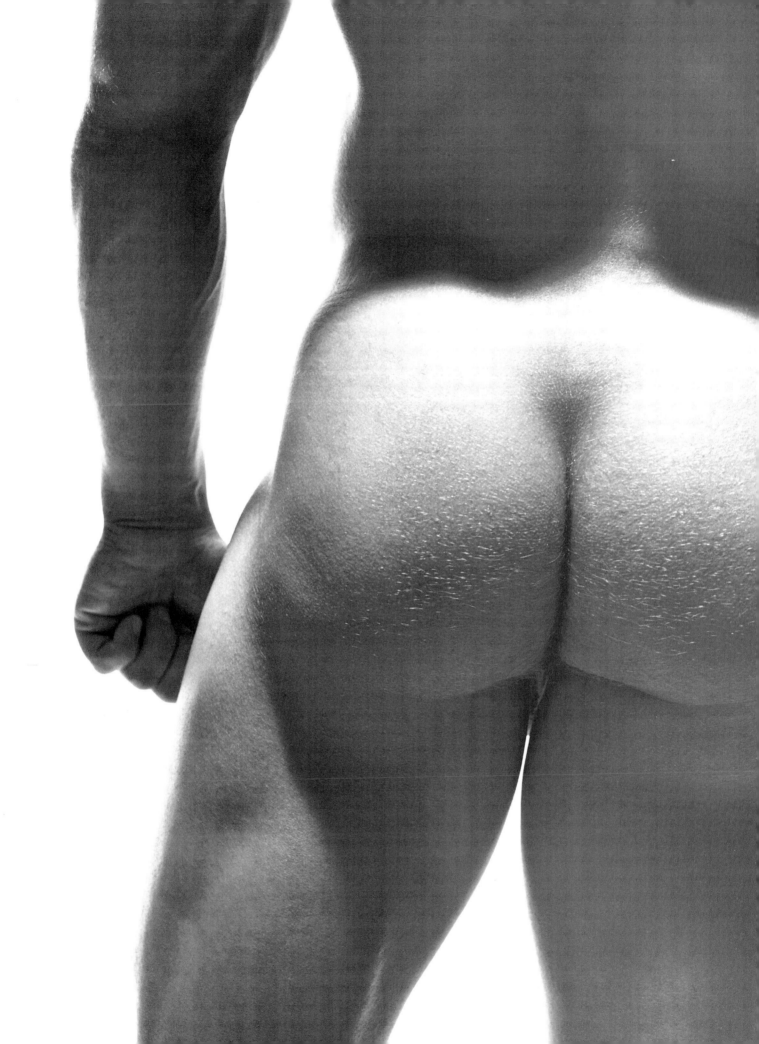

BUTTOCKS

The glutes (gluteus maximus and gluteus medius) are the largest muscle group in the body (for everyone) and easily incorporate other muscle groups to participate in the workload. By strengthening this group of muscles you will add power to your jumps, strength to your cycling, and youth as a sign that follows you. Think about it, after you reach a certain age, no specifics but let's just say it isn't 17, there comes a time when you check yourself out in the mirror at home after a shower and wonder if your butt fell off in the shower. I vowed that it would never happen to me, but as I write this book, sitting on my behind in front of this computer, I feel the spread. It seems not only to spread wider but it can also redistribute itself into your back; a friend of mine says he has two butts on his back. I know exactly what he's talking about. The following exercises will build strength and firm the muscles and restore a bit of youth in your walk.

STANDING LEG RAISES

The use of a chair or wall will provide you with balance and stabilization so use the prop until you have mastered your balance; however a chair can be used whenever you want. Stand next to the chair and hold on to the back with a easy grip. Use your central position to mark your body position. Keep your body lifted and think about where you feel this exercise.

Allow one foot to rotate about 20 percent, shifting the toe position out and keeping your heels together. Slowly slide your foot back and lift your leg off the floor, right behind you; after all, that's what we are working, the behind. You will feel your buttocks take over and sustain the leg as it travels through space; your buttocks will feel the work primarily in the upper part of the butt. This is called the gluteus medius; that part, I often remind people, is your youth.

Lower the leg back to the start position and repeat as many times as you have set. Try not to swing the leg back and forth, and always maintain your central position. This will keep the work in the buttocks and will give you the results you desire. Remember, this is the last part of your body that leaves a room. Think about it.

PRONE LEG CROSS RAISES (L-SHAPED LEG)

Get down on the floor on your hands and knees, as you did for the hamstring exercises you learned before. Keep your hands open and your elbows soft. The reason for the word *soft* is to remind you not to lock out your joint and put undue stress on your important and most-abused joints (elbows, knees, shoulders). Keep your shoulders relaxed and away from your ears, very similar to the push-up position. Tighten the middle of the body to get you into the central position and elevate one leg into the air with an L shape to it. You are going to lower your leg toward the floor, but instead of going in a direct downward line, bring the knee in so that the knee touches the calf of the support leg. Just bring it down slowly and tap the top of the calf and then raise it back up. Hold the torso firm so that the spine re-mains straight and the body stays parallel to the floor. This is vital to the effectiveness of the exercise. Once you lose this key position, the exercise will lose its intensity and the chance of the muscles in the back taking on unnecessary work increases.

Continue to lower and lift the L-shaped leg, tapping the calf until you have met your goal, and repeat on the other side. After finishing a set on each leg, rest a bit and sit back to stretch.

SIDE-LYING LEG RAISES

Now you get to lie on the floor, so get down there and take advantage of the fact that this is permitted. When you are on the floor, lying on your side, the most common mistake that I see is that the alignment of the spine seems to be ignored because people think that if they are on the floor they are supported. It is like assuming any plank over a body of water will support weight in its center like a bridge that is carefully engineered and built. You must think and maintain the awareness of your central position even when lying on your side. As you lie on your side, try to keep your waistline off the floor. Even the fittest will find this a helpful tool to boost and benefit their technique.

Lie on your side and lift your waist up so there is a space that you can feel with your fingers. Then rest your hand in front of you so that your body weight doesn't shift from front to back. This start position is very much like a sleeping position. Hands rest under your head as a pil-low would, and your knees are bent at a 45-degree angle, the leg on top stacked on top of the leg on the floor. Bring your legs forward so that they are in front of you a little, just so you are not fully extended on the floor. This will help stabilize your entire body.

Before anything, raise the foot on top away from the foot on the floor. You can see in the photo illustration that it is only a couple inches. Your heel will be higher than your toes. Just by getting into this position you should feel the exercise. Now lift the top leg up, leading with the heel. This will be felt on the side of the thigh and most of all in the buttocks. Lower to where you started and lift again. Repeat as many as your set requires, and then stretch the muscle by lying on the floor with your legs crossed. Flip over and do the same on the other leg, and so on. Just keep the focus on the buttocks and the central position.

SUPINE TILT
(ONE LEG UP)

Now you are on your back. The entire upper body rests during this exercise, but the torso and the lower body have work ahead. Lie on the floor with both knees bent and your feet flat, arms relaxed and hands resting beside you with your palms down. Your feet should be about six inches away from your hands on the floor.

Extend one leg up into the air and point the toes toward the ceiling a bit; don't overdo this. You have to hold this leg up in the air the entire set, so you can also figure if you need to modify, just bend the knee or cross the leg over the one on the floor. Keeping the extended leg elevated, push from the foot on the floor to elevate your buttocks and lower back off the floor. You will exhale as you lift here in order to protect the spine and to ensure proper form. Lift up to the point where your body is resting on your upper back and shoulders, the entire midsection lifted. In physical therapy circles they call this a "bridge." Inhale as you lower yourself down and then lift again, using the breath as you did before to assist. You will feel this in the hamstrings and the buttock on the side that has the foot on the floor. Your elevated leg is resting—believe it or not. Continue until you finish your repetitions and then switch legs. A stretch may be necessary after each leg; this exercise is strenuous. Simply extend the leg

worked into the air as if you were about to perform a set of the tilt, and pull back on the leg. You will feel a great stretch in the hamstrings and buttocks.

LEG RAISE

This exercise will resemble exercises you may have seen where a man, using a Roman chair, positions himself on the device with his feet clamped into the apparatus, hips resting on a pad, and his body dangling in front without support. He lowers his upper body and then swings his body upward, arching his back, and then down again. The benefits are great, but that exercise isn't for everyone.

To modify the exercise, I have reversed the end of the body that moves through gravity. This is one way you can strengthen your lower back and your buttocks without the risks connected with such exercises as the one on the Roman chair. Don't misunderstand: I think the exercise involving the Roman chair has benefits for those who are trained to that level. By working in the reverse I think that I can bring you the same benefits with fewer risks.

You can use a chair as is represented in the photographs or a bench as long as when you are resting on the bench, your knees can rest on the floor without having to reach for the floor. Get a bench or chair that isn't too high.

Rest your body over the chair so that your sternum and pelvis are touching the edges. The "core" of your body will hold you on the surface and your limbs will do the work. Take your hands down and hold on to the legs of the chair; if you are on a bench, bring your hands to the bench right above your head and hold the pad. Your legs are resting on the floor, knees and feet in contact with the floor. This is your starting position. Inhale, and as you exhale squeeze your buttocks together and lift both legs at least five inches off the floor. Hold for a second, and then return your legs and feet to the floor. This is not a contest to see how high you can go; it is a strengthening exercise that will work your buttocks and legs. Start by doing just a few reps at first. If the bench or chair is uncomfortable because of your penis and balls, you can put a towel on the chair to cushion that area. It doesn't have to be uncomfortable, and if it is you will have an excuse to stop doing it. Don't stop!

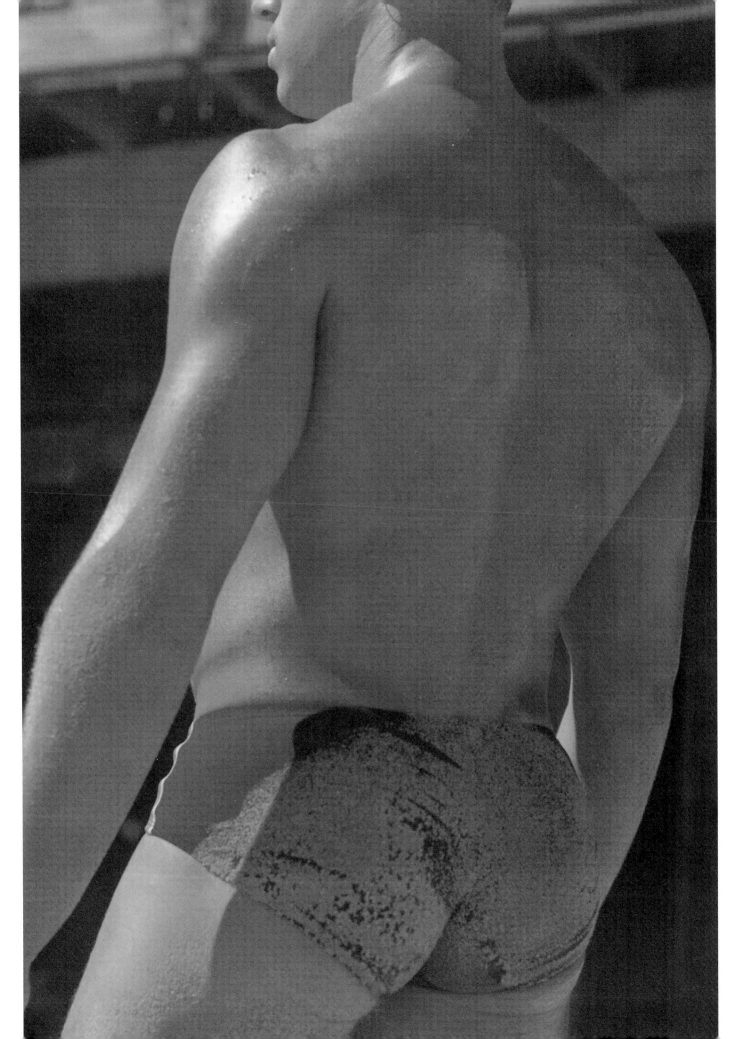

Core Training

The core of your body is like the core of an apple: the center, the middle, the root. The core incorporates the abdominals and the lower back. The key to a well-rounded fitness routine is to pay specific attention to the core muscle groups so that the core can support all the other demands you are putting on your system: muscular, cardiovascular, and the all-important flexibility component.

We all have them and yet when we see the washboards that grace these pages as well as the men who have put in the hours, weeks, and years to get them that way, we get defensive and outright nasty. The truth is that we all have the same basic structure to our abdominals, which are often confused with the stomach. The stomach digests your food, but if you're not careful your abdominals will wear your food. Everyone's rectus abdominus supports the upper body from the lower body, connects the two parts of the body together, and holds all of the organs in their respective places. Your abs are shaped like an accordion; yes, an accordion! This muscle has the ability to expand and shorten like no other muscle in the body and features wormlike indentations. That's what you see when a man or woman has that "six-pack" look. The reason you can see their definition is because they have reduced the fat in front of the muscle and developed musculature that is the envy of the masses.

Many people refer to the upper and lower abs. These are just the areas in which the muscle is located, toward the upper and lower ends of the same muscle. Your rectus abdominus is one muscle and should always be considered as such. Specific exercises can be performed to enlist the action from either the top or the bottom part of the muscle. The sides are another group, called obliques. Refer to the anatomy photo illustration on page 22 to see where everything sits.

CRUNCHES

Research has proven that the crunch is the most effective exercise to strengthen the abdominals. The crunch is superior to the full sit-up. If you have ever done a set of full sit-ups, you can understand why the crunch is a more reasonable exercise, with the same benefit. Variations of this theme will also provide excellent benefits, but if you are just starting, then the crunch is ideal. (See pages 58 and 59 in the Ideals section.)

Start on the floor, on your back with both legs bent. Keeping your feet firmly planted on the floor, be aware that your back should be stable and steady. You can start by elevating your shoulders off the floor and grasping your thighs. You have anchored yourself into a position that will introduce you to your own six-pack. Hold on to this for just a few seconds; the weight of your head will start to make your neck uncomfortable. Bring your arms up beside your head and hold your head with each hand independent from one another. Inhale deeply, and as you exhale lift your shoulders up, clearing the floor by squeezing the midsection and holding your lower body down. You should feel your ribcage sliding down toward your pelvis and the shortening of the muscle in the front of your body. Lower your back, inhaling as you do.

The most effective breathing happens when there is the least amount of room in the lungs to breathe, so it is natural for you to breathe out as you lift up. Always try to maintain enough space between the chin and the chest to ensure that your air passages are open. Repeat the same contraction to complete the goal you have set for yourself and you will see how quickly you will feel and see some results.

REVERSE CURLS

This is the crunch backward. As stated above, the abdominal muscle functions from both ends of the muscle. The reverse curl will help you connect the sensation in the lower area of the abs. This area is problematic for many people because they just cannot sense the work in the muscle. This exercise will help you do just that, and it will help you get stronger.

I put a towel in between the knees so that the legs have a task to perform, forcing them to participate rather than just go along for the ride. Just bunch up a towel or roll it nicely and pinch it between your knees. Hold the towel with comfortable pressure, not too tight.

Lift your feet off the floor and continue to hold the towel between the knees. If you find the towel uncomfortable, remove it and master the reverse curl with your legs alone. Hold your legs in a 45-degree bent position and bring your hands behind your head, as you did with the crunch. Keep your head and shoulders on the floor the entire time so that you can emphasize the lower area of the abdominals.

Bring your legs back as a unit, so that your tailbone lifts off the floor because it has to. This is a teaching exercise, so learn about the way the lower part of the abs pulls with the assistance of the hips and how the muscle has to pull downward into the floor, in order to get the legs to go where you want them. Gradually allow your legs to go back to the starting position, and then pull again. As you pull the legs in you should exhale and feel how the breathing helps specifically with this action. It will help you lock the muscle into the work, and the results are awesome. After your set, bring your knees into your chest and stretch before you move on.

CRUNCH WITH TOWEL

This is a combination of the two previous exercises; you need the assistance of the towel this time. Press the towel between your legs and keep your feet together on the floor. This will stabilize your lower body and offer the inner-thigh muscles the opportunity to be involved and active while working the abs. When exercising the abdominal wall, we concentrate primarily on the muscles leading to the pelvis; therefore, the muscles that make up the adductors (inner thigh) should be recruited to take some of the pressure off of the hip.

Hold on to the towel with your hands held behind your head. Inhale first and then exhale and contract the abs, lifting the upper body enough to clear the shoulder blades and add the pressure of the inner-thigh contraction to the intensity. Work slowly and really feel the work in the muscle. Release the contraction slowly, and then hit it again. Keep your focus on the breath and the surface of your body. This muscle is used all the time, to sit, to stand, to walk, to balance, and to twist. By strengthening the abdominal muscle, you help it function better and with more efficiency.

To me, the obliques—the muscles that wrap around your torso—are one of the sexiest muscle groups in the body. They run diagonally in two directions (internal and external) and assist you with bending and supporting the all-important spine and posture. The fingerlike muscle that you see on many men is the seratus, which needs to be contracted or stimulated with a pulling action. (See the Pull-up in the Ideals for this group.)

CROSSOVER

Get into crunch position: on your back, feet flat on the floor, with your hands behind your head. Remember to keep your hands separate and the buttocks tight, so that your back remains on the floor. The crossover will allow you to work on one side at a time. Start with the right side by lifting only the left elbow up. The directions you want to create are upward, then diagonal from the center, looking at the opposite knee in front of you, then back to center, and release. It will be performed in four stages for the learning process and then made into one smooth movement.

Stabilize your lower body and inhale to prepare for the contraction; then as you exhale a little of the air, lift up and crossover to the side, finishing the exhalation. Return to the middle and relax. Perform even numbers of repetitions on both sides of the body and then rest. To stretch the body, lie flat on the floor, body, including arms and legs, fully extended. Reach so that you feel your entire body pull from both ends and so that you never felt longer in your life. If you hold that and breathe freely, your body will stretch nicely.

FISHHOOK

This exercise attacks the side of the body and will be a great addition to a well-established routine. The notion of the hook implies the shape, similar to that of the letter J.

First, begin in the starting crunch position, lying on your back, feet flat on the floor, hands behind the head. Extend one hand at your side, next to your hip and about an inch off the floor. Here is where this exercise differs from the others. Inhale and elevate your upper body; as you exhale slowly, lock into position, and then reach with your extended arm toward your foot, shaving the floor underneath you with your back as you complete the exhalation. Return to the center position and then release back down to the floor, inhaling as you relax. Remember the hook element of the exercise is like skimming your back along the floor, or like spreading peanut butter on bread. You must sustain the upper-body position in order to feel the full effect. Continue with your set number and then switch to the other side.

BACK FLEX

This is similar to body surfing, but without the water. The strength of the lower back can be found in many of the exercises in this book; however, sometimes there is an exercise that can isolate a specific muscle group that needs special attention. This is that exercise. By strengthening the lower back you encourage the entire core of the body to find balance and symmetry. If you work on your crunches without paying attention to your back, the imbalance will creep up on you one day when you can't get out of bed because of the pain.

Lie on your stomach on the floor, with your head slightly lifted. Bring your hands under your hips so your pelvis won't grind into the floor. Keep your feet apart a little and get ready. Inhale through your mouth and nose and lift both feet and shoulders off the floor, squeezing the buttocks and the lower-back muscles to hold you in this position for five seconds. Exhale as you release. Breathing in the reverse order will make this isometric contraction difficult.

ERECTOR SPINAE

The lower back needs strength-building exercise just as does any other part of the body, maybe even more. But you must realize that the demands on the lower back are enormous, and therefore any exercise should be smart and effective. This is not a body part you want to build; this is preventive fitness. In order to maintain the body's balance, you must work opposing muscle groups. The lower back is in direct competition with the abdominals; if you work out one side you should exercise the other. It's only fair.

Many lower-back problems come from overuse of the hip flexor, combined with weak abdominal muscles. By strengthening the abs and stretching the hip flexors, any work that you offer your lower back will be well worth it. My own experience with back pain has turned me into an advocate for lower-back health and maintenance. If you suffer from occasional back pain, you know what it means to feel crooked and uncomfortable.

Stretching

Stretching should be a part of every activity, be it exercise or a sport activity. Gentle stretching can be performed in just a few minutes and prep your body for the stresses it will encounter while you are pushing and pulling or running and jumping. Stretch every time, at the beginning and end of each session, and make it a habit.

Each stretch should be performed without bouncing or jerking, which can possibly injure you. Holding a stretch for about 15 to 30 seconds will stimulate the stretch response and allow the muscles to lengthen properly. Feel the tension in the muscle without excessive pain. Never attempt to stretch muscles beyond their normal range of motion.

The stretches that follow, done together or separately, will benefit your mental setup for a workout or a game. Stretch the muscles that will be used in the activity, and as you stretch set up a mental plan as to how you will play, how hard you want to train that day, or how badly you want to win. These few minutes can result in a sense of empowerment that many of us take for granted. Stretch the body and the imagination. Stretching routines for warming up and for cooling down will follow the text and photo illustrations.

STANDARD STRETCHES FOR GOOD HEALTH

LOW-BACK STRETCH (STANDING)

Anyone who suffers from lower-back pain will agree that the discomfort can be unbearable. This stretch may offer you relief and by applying it to your regular routine, you can reduce the onset of lower-back pain in the future. The photograph demonstrates how this low-back stretch can be performed holding onto a railing or post.

Stand at arm's distance from a railing or post. A chair could slide and you could fall back onto the floor, so use something that is stable. Separate your feet wider than your shoulders, turning your toes out a bit. Grasp the railing and squat down. With the support of your midsection (core), you should maintain proper posture and alignment of your spine. Allow your head to extend from your neck naturally, keeping your eyes focused on the floor. This position resembles the form a diver would be in just before he jumps off the board into the pool. Your body weight should rest back. The stretch will be felt through the side of the upper back and the arms as well.

Inhale a full breath and prepare to exhale. As you breathe out, lift your middle back, arching upward like an angry cat. It should be like hollowing out your abs or pulling a string up through your torso, lifting upward until you feel the stretch in your lower back. Allow your neck to relax and your head to drop gradually, pulling your chin in comfortably. The pull should be felt the entire length of the back, but primarily in the triangle area, just above the buttocks. Return to the flat-back position and repeat this stretch. If you don't have a railing or post, try a doorknob on an open door.

If you choose not to use a support or prop, squat down again into your tackle position. Take hold of your thighs using your hands, holding the meaty part of the side of the thigh. Your seated position should not exceed 90 degrees, so don't sit down too low. Holding the weight in your legs, lift through the spine as described above and breathe out as you hollow out the abs. Release the head as described above and enjoy the stretch.

QUAD AND HIP-FLEXOR STRETCH

Stand next to a chair or in a doorway, somewhere you can support and balance yourself. Use the support until you have mastered your balance and can feel the benefit of this important stretch.

Bend both knees slightly to unlock the knee joint and release the stress from the lower back. Bend either your right or left leg until you can reach and hold your foot with your hand on the same side (right hand / right leg—left hand / left leg). Maintain your natural posture at all times and focus on the tension you feel in your thighs. In this position you may want to arch your back a bit— this is due to inflexibility and tight muscles. The hip flexor gets overused in daily life as well as in fitness activities, so the hips and legs demand serious attention.

While holding on to the foot, concentrate on the support of the abdominals and upper body. Try not to crouch over, which would limit the effectiveness of the stretch. Relax your shoulders and focus your eyes in front of you. Contract or squeeze your buttock muscles and feel the pressure in the front of your leg—the quadriceps muscle. This contraction forces the stretch to go a little deeper and to the root of muscle. Hold that position for 15 to 30 seconds and slowly release your foot back down to the floor. Shake your leg out a bit and then perform the same stretch on the other side with the other leg. Everything remains the same—just pay attention and feel the release.

HAMSTRING STRETCH

Prop your leg up on a railing, chair, bench or even just in front of you on the floor. Depending on your level of flexibility the position will vary. Try to extend your leg so that it is straight and there is no bend in the knee. Be aware of your posture and try not to let your shoulders round over. You upper torso should also face the leg that is extended with squared-off shoulders and firm abdominals. For some, this will be enough. You should feel tension in the back of your leg, all the way up to your buttocks. Pull your toes toward your body to enhance the stretch.

To advance this stretch you can simply reach your hands forward toward your foot, maintaining your upper body position. And to further advance this stretch, rotate your upper body to the front and raise one arm above your head. Not only will you feel more tension through the leg you are stretching, you will also feel the side of your body (the same side as the raised arm) lengthen and stretch. Hold the stretch for 15 seconds or so and repeat on the other side.

TRICEP STRETCH

Standing tall in a natural postural position, extend one arm above your head and bend at the elbow, allowing your hand to rest behind the neck. Take the other hand and touch your bent elbow and begin to feel the stretch behind the arm in the triceps muscles. Pull your abs in so that you are standing without bending or leaning. Gently pull on your elbow enough to feel the tension in the muscle a little bit more and hold for about 15 seconds. Release the arm back down to your side and repeat on the other side. It may take you awhile to get your arm up over your head, but that should show you just how much you need this stretch.

BACK-SHOULDER STRETCH

This area of the back is very difficult to stretch due primarily to poor technique and misunderstanding of the arm and the shoulder position. Even when stretching, you should be conscious of posture and alignment.

To begin this stretch, stand up tall and separate your feet to a natural standing position with your arms resting at your sides. Take one arm and raise it in front of you to chest level. Bring that arm across your body until it is pointing to the side and grasp it with your free hand at the elbow. Gently pull your elbow across the chest until you feel tension in the back of your shoulder. The

most important thing to remember here is to keep your shoulder down, away from the head, and relaxed. Repeat using the other arm.

CHEST STRETCH

Using a railing (as seen in the demonstration) or perhaps a doorway to assist with this stretch will help you achieve the length your chest needs. You need to hold something at about waist level or just a bit higher in order to keep the stretch effective. Facing away from the railing so that your buttocks touch the railing, take your hands back and grasp the railing gently with your fingers rotated outward. Hold on to the railing and step forward a full step, keeping your hands where they were to start with. You will feel a pulling in the chest muscles. Try not to lean forward or back too much; you want the chest to open and receive the stretch, not to compromise your posture. Lift your chest up and lift your chin slightly. Try not to drop your head back for any stretching exercise.

If using a doorway, just hold the frame of the door and perform the same position by stepping through the doorway and holding on to the frame with both hands. This is not a competition, so try not to overdo the stretch. Your muscles need to stretch in order to free the body from the continuous shortening of all the muscle groups. If we didn't stretch we would most likely bend over, have sunken chests and poor posture, which would lead to lower back pain and so on. Flexibility is a vital component to your overall health, a major part of the foundation of a complete fitness program.

NECK RELIEVER (NOT SHOWN)

Many people suffer from stiffness in the upper part of their backs and from tight traps, which sometimes limit the range of motion around the neck. There are many common activities that cause this area of the body to become stressed and strained: holding a telephone receiver with the shoulder and head, sleeping incorrectly, a past injury, high stress or anxiety. No matter what the reason, this stretch will offer you some relief.

Stand with your hands at your sides. Bring one hand behind you and rest the back side of your hand on your buttocks, while the other arm bends at the elbow and reaches for the wrist of the resting arm. Hold the wrist with your hand and keep the extended arm down. You should feel a slight stretch begin in the shoulder of the extended arm. Allow your head to drop away gently from that extended arm and feel the tension from the ear to the outer edge of the shoulder. You can allow your head to roll forward a bit, but try to give this stretch the benefit of happening. Return to your standing position with your arms at your side; switch arms and repeat, using the other arm. This should offer you some relief and can be done anywhere.

HALF-MOON

This is one of those statuesque poses that feels good and helps you focus on your feelings and balance. The trick is to think of yourself as a sculpture; that type of mental suggestion will help you feel the stretch more effectively.

Stand tall with natural posture, keeping your feet together and your shoulders relaxed. With your arms extended, lift your arms out to the side and raise them above your head with your palms pressed together. Lace your fingers together with your index fingers pointing straight up into the air above you. Feel as though your arms are being pulled upward, lengthening through the entire body. Arch to one side slowly with control and mental awareness. Allow the side of the body to stretch as well as the underarm, hip, and lower back. You will feel the tension most where the body rotates, at the waistline. When you think about it, this is the area of the body that supports most of the upper body all the time you are standing and sitting. Hold for 15 seconds and then return to the starting position. Release your arms for a moment and then raise them up again and perform the same stretch on the other side. Remember to focus on the space in front of you and let yourself relax and enjoy this one.

STRETCHES FOR WARMING UP AND COOLING DOWN

INNER-THIGH STRETCH

Separate your feet wider than your shoulders, turning your toes out a little. Bend down into your knees and come down into a squat position. This position reminds me of the defensive line of a football team. Lower down and rest your elbows on your legs and hold your abdominals firm. This will help you reduce the risk of undue stress in the lower back. Distribute your weight evenly through your feet and focus on your balance. You should feel the stretch in the inner thighs, a pull from the groin down through the thigh to the knee. Feel this sensation for about 15 seconds. Then, ever so slightly, lift your hips up by extending both legs. You will feel a pull in the hamstrings, the muscles behind your thighs. Then return to your tackle position, the squat position. Take your elbows to the inside of your knee joints and press out against each knee. You should feel the stretch again in the inner thighs. Hold this for 10 seconds and then return to the standing position.

HAMSTRING STRETCH WITH TOWEL

Using a towel for this stretch will help you increase your flexibility in the back of your leg and allow you to keep your upper body relaxed and down on the floor. Lie down on the floor on your back with both feet on the floor, knees bent. Pull one knee in toward the chest and place the towel onto the ball of your foot. This towel position is vital for the effectiveness of the stretch.

Lift your foot, with the towel, into the air and extend your leg as much as you can while holding on to the ends of the towel. Keep your leg in the air and feel the stretch start to pull the back of your leg, the hamstring. Keep extending your leg until your leg is straight. If this is extremely difficult, bend the knee a bit and work on your flexibility more often.

If your leg is extended fully, pull gently on the towel to enhance the stretch and you will feel the stretch's intensity become greater. The towel helps your upper body maintain better spinal alignment and thus will serve the muscles that this stretch is intended for. Hold the stretch for 30 seconds, then bend the knee and remove the towel from your toe. Repeat the same stretch on the other leg and remember to breathe throughout the process.

LOWER-BACK STRETCH
(ON FLOOR)

Lie down on the floor with your knees bent and your feet resting on the floor. Pull your knees into your chest by holding on to your thighs, behind the knee joint. It is important not to pull on the shin part of your leg as a protection to the knee joint itself. You should feel the stretch in your lower back and buttocks muscles. Contract your abdominals (pull them in) and feel your legs come in a bit more. Hold this for about 30 seconds and try to keep your neck and upper shoulder area relaxed and your breathing easy. Roll up to a sitting position with the help of holding on to your legs and move on.

QUAD STRETCH (FACE DOWN)

This is the same stretch you mastered standing up, only you are lying face down on the floor. Take hold of one foot with your hand and pull your foot toward your buttocks. You will feel the tension in the front of your leg and in the upper part of the hip. You will also feel the front of your shoulder stretch a bit because of the position your arm is in. Hold the position for 30 seconds or so and repeat on the other leg.

CALF STRETCH

The mechanics of the calf are vital to perform any task, be it athletic or ordinary daily activities. As with any of the parts of the body that depend on rotations and flexion, it is wise and highly recommended to prepare the calves for the weight load and the activity you are involving them in.

This stretch requires a prop that will support your feet. A step on a staircase, the leg of the bench you are using (if it allows you to position your foot), a curb, or even a wall will do fine. Place the balls of your feet on the prop of choice with the heels hanging over the edge. You can rest your hands on a wall or at your side, but continue supporting your body with a tall chest and good posture. Allow your heels to come down and begin to feel the stretch in the lower calf; the tension should be felt immediately.

Hold this position for 15 to 30 seconds. Try not to force the stretch if the muscle won't react. You can also perform this stretch one foot at a time if that will help you balance.

WARM-UP STRETCH ROUTINE

A good five-minute warm-up: Start by jogging in place for a minute, or doing 30 jumping jacks. Circle your arms and rotate your torso from side to side to get your blood flowing. This will raise your body temperature, distribute blood throughout the body, and lubricate the joints of the shoulders, hips, and knees. Any movement will be better than starting out cold.

jog or march in place	**5 minutes**
inner-thigh stretch	**15 seconds**
lower-back stretch (standing or floor)	**30 seconds**
hamstring stretch (standing or floor)	**60 seconds (30 sec each side)**
quad stretch (standing or floor)	**60 seconds (30 sec each side)**
calf stretch	**15 seconds**
half-moon	**60 seconds (30 sec each side)**

COOL-DOWN STRETCHES

Your cooling-down period should be a time to acknowledge your output and gains. Realize the amount of work you did and how you feel. The stretching portion at the end of your workout or activity is a reinforcement that we can give ourselves. The stretches should reflect the muscle groups that you hit, but in the scheme of things a good cool-down will consist of the following stretches.

back-shoulder stretch	**60 seconds (30 sec each side)**
chest stretch	**30 seconds**
quad stretch (floor)	**60 seconds (30 sec each side)**
hamstring stretch (floor)	**60 seconds (30 sec each side)**
lower-back stretch (floor)	**60 seconds**

Try to implement these stretches into your sport activities as well. You may feel that they look stupid in front of your friends, but you might set an example. You can also perform these stretches in the locker room or away from everyone else. They only take a few minutes and your body will benefit greatly.

Rehabilitation Exercises

LOWER BACK

The lower back is the most common area for stress and pain. There are two remedies to help you out of the agony of lower back pain: strengthening your abdominals, as I have shown you in the Core exercises, and stretching and strengthening the muscles that cause the painful effects of back discomfort.

HIP-FLEXOR STRETCH

Stand next to a bench, step, chair, ledge, or surface that is at least 12 inches off the floor. Bring your left foot up onto the platform, making sure that your entire foot rests on the platform. Step the right foot back quite a bit, and position it parallel to the other foot. You will feel a calf stretch already. If you'd like, you could hold that for a second and enjoy.

Lift up onto the toes of the right foot and balance as well as you can. It will help to focus your eyes in front of you and think about your position. Keep your shoulders lifted and begin to feel the stretch in your right hip. Draw your right hand forward and lift it in front of you, then upward into the air above you. Feel the extension of the arm pull up through your abs and then squeeze your buttocks together and hold your focus. This stretch will be felt in the hip area, next to your groin. Hold on to the stretch for 15 seconds at least and then relax back down and bring your foot off the platform. Switch legs and perform the stretch on the left side with the left foot on the floor. Then repeat the stretch on the right foot again and you are done.

Point of interest. Dr. Richard Bachrach, a leading osteopathic sports doctor in New York City, believes that stretching the right hip flexor (right foot on floor), then the left side, and then the right side again leads to a better balanced stretch for lower back pain. Here's why. We live in a predominantly right-handed world, and most left-handed people will understand what this means. The result is that the right sides of our bodies are challenged more often than the left. This creates stress and imbalance. Most people with lower-back pain find the pain more often than not on the right side of their lower backs. Therefore, Bachrach believes, stretching the right side of the body twice *will relieve and correct the imbalance that the environment places on our bodies. He doesn't blame the world—he just wants to heal it!*

SHIN SPLINTS

If you are a runner, jogger, tennis player, or participate in aerobics classes and step classes, you may experience shin splints, the tight and often painful tension in the front of the lower leg. The tibialis anterior is a thin, shear muscle that extends from the knee to the ankle. Shin splints are painful to the touch, limit the range of motion of the ankle, and make your run or whatever activity you do less intense.

TAPS (NOT SHOWN)

This quick and effective exercise, which will ease the stress in front and build strength, is simple to do. Standing or sitting, put a light weight on the top of your foot, right on top of the toes. You could use a broomstick, an ankle weight, something that will create resistance for this forgotten muscle. Now lift your toes into the air, keeping your heel on the floor. This type of flexion is called dorsi flexion; it causes the foot to lift up toward the leg. Lower the weight with ease and repeat 8 to 12 times on each foot per set. You could perform two sets and feel the benefits. This exercise, while promoting strength and balance to a forgotten area of the leg, also provides the ankle with a smart exercise.

ROTATOR CUFF

The rotator cuff is a powerful group of muscles and connecting tendons that attach your upper arm to your shoulder blade. It helps you reach, push, pull, throw, and lift. Without it, your shoulder would be virtually useless.

An injury to the rotator cuff can be caused by falling on your shoulder, straining by doing too much lifting and reaching, or even twisting your shoulder during an exercise class or weight-lifting session. Even daily activities like yard work, cleaning out the garage, or taking on a new activity can trigger pain. Age can also play a part due to the fact that your muscles get weaker as you age, unless you maintain an exercise program diligently.

Sometimes it can be difficult to know if a rotator cuff injury is in fact what you are suffering from. An injury to your rotator cuff can make everyday activities such as reaching overhead, scratching your back, washing your hair, sleeping on your shoulder, or even carrying a bag uncomfortable and painful.

If your injury isn't severe, all you may need to do is heal your injury with rest and patience. Here are two methods to stretch and strengthen your arm in a way that will help your shoulder gain flexibility and strength.

TOWEL STRETCH

Stand up tall holding on to a towel with your "good" hand, the side that is not experiencing pain. Place the back of the hand on your injured or sore side across your back, just above your buttocks. With your good hand, drape the towel over your good shoulder and grab it with the hand behind you (see photo on page 133). Gently pull on the towel with your good arm, elevating your injured arm slowly. Lift the arm behind as high as you can comfortably and hold it for about five seconds. Pull the towel in the other direction, letting it scratch your shoulder as it would if you were drying your back after a shower, and repeat the stretch six to eight times.

Take your time and build up to the point where you can hold the stretch for 10 to 60 seconds and /or pull your arm higher behind you. I would also encourage you to do this exercise on the other side of the body, just to promote healthy shoulders and reduce the risks of injuries in the future.

THE BAND

Holding on to an elastic band, available at any sporting-goods store, position your arm in the shape of an L, with your elbows touching your sides. Your palms should be facing up and the elastic band held firmly. Slowly rotate one hand outward, away from the midline of your body, like a door on hinges, and release. The resistance you feel should be in the side of your shoulder. Take your time with this and maintain the position of your elbow against your body at all times. You can perform this exercise one arm at a time or with both arms rotating out at the same time. As you rotate, count to eight slowly to help you reduce your speed in both directions and allow the resistance to be felt.

Knees are abused and used in almost everything we do. They are strong enough to support unbelievable weight loads, run endless miles, jump to new heights, yet the knee is a fragile joint. The intricate anatomy of the knee, when studied and understood, should baffle and amaze you. How can it support what it does, how can we require it to do what we do, and then take for granted that it will always be there for us? But what happens when we have knee pain and a possible injury? It is unbearable and nagging and debilitating.

Knee injuries can occur during sport activities like football, hockey, or tennis as well as during repeated impact activities like aerobics, running, or cycling. A knee injury can also occur in an accident or fall. When you have a knee injury you know it. You will feel it almost every time you move your leg.

One method to help treat a sore knee is to brace the knee while you exercise and even when you are mobile in your daily life. It is not worth the pain you may have later if you don't pay attention to your knee when it hurts. Braces are sold at pharmacies and sporting-good stores everywhere. Try not to let your ego win over being practical and safe.

EXTENSIONS

Another method to ensure a healthy knee is simply to strengthen the area

around the joint itself. Lie down flat on the floor with both legs extended. Bend the good leg at the knee and set your foot down. Keep your buttocks and your hands down on the floor and hold your midsection firm. With the other leg, "the bad one," lift up in the extended position until your knees are side by side. Then stop and hold for a second. Slowly lower the same leg until you are about one inch from the floor. Lift up again and repeat to complete a set of 12. Then rest and repeat the set three times. This exercise will be felt along the front of the thigh, from the knee to the hip. Strengthening the muscle without bending the hinge that is irritated will promote the strength of the muscle attached to the joint and relieve some of the discomfort.

CHAPTER SEVEN

Developing an Aerobics Program

Aerobic training requires the same mental consciousness and shares the same principles with regard to frequency (times per week), duration (time per session), and intensity (load) that strength training does. To measure whether your aerobic training program is creating change and whether your body is adapting to the work, you can look in the mirror, step on a scale, tighten your belt, or measure your resting heart rate and your exercise heart rate. Heart-rate monitoring is a vital component of serious cardiovascular training programs. Heart-rate monitoring provides numbers and measurements of change and progress. Your body (heart included) will adapt to most any program and then level off. This means that you need to change the program to see additional benefits and measure your progress.

The transition from one exercise routine to the next can challenge the body and re-create the soreness you experienced the first time around. You are fitter than you once were, but the new stress you are demanding of your body causes it to rethink and perform the new task with some coordination challenges and fatigue. Your body is just telling you to slow down a little until it can perform the way you want it to.

Let your body get used to the new program and activity. Give it the opportunity to feel the moves and get into the rhythm. The physiological demands are the same as they were the first time you started, and the reaction is the same, no matter how fit you are. The best example is the beautifully built guy, with all the muscles any man would want, who walks into an aerobics class thinking that he can run circles around all the women jumping or stepping up on those benches. Ten minutes into the class the guy is huffing and puffing and staggering toward the exit. He looks fit, but there is always room to improve. The truth of the matter is you are never really done. There is no finish line when it comes to fitness.

When you change your routine, you should reduce your intensity level a little until you get used to the work. It can be defeating not to succeed at something you yourself initiated. There is no law saying that you have to stay with an activity that you hate. Do something you like, but do it intelligently. Then do it well. Then change it again.

Specific stretches are good for one activity but may not target other muscles for other activities. A runner wouldn't stretch the same muscles a swimmer would. A tennis player wouldn't stretch the same muscles a weight lifter would. There are certain stretches for every sport. Find the appropriate stretches for your sport, and when your program evolves, let your flexibility routine change as well.

SERIOUS STUFF

To develop and maintain cardiorespiratory fitness and body composition in healthy adults, the American College of Sport Medicine recommends the following:

1. Training three to five days a week = Frequency of Training.

2. Training at 60 to 90 percent of maximum heart rate (220 − age = max HR) = Intensity of Training.

3. Continuous aerobic activity for 15 to 60 minutes = Duration of Training (depending on the intensity level of the activity). Low-intensity activities should be conducted for a longer period of time to achieve total fitness. This type of training is recommended for the nonathletic adult.

4. Activity choices involve any activity that uses large muscle groups in a sustained and continuous nature. Most of these activities are rhythmic and repetitive; for example, swimming, cycling, running, rowing, jumping rope, walking, hiking, skating.

DAILY ACTIVITIES

For many men, the choice of exercise options is not a positive choice but one of confusion and frustration. Which activity you choose can affect the success and the commitment you make for the future of your routine as well as the enjoyment you get from that routine. Men have a tendency to

take on assignments and have the choices made for them when they are unsure or unfamiliar with the consequences or the results. Men will rely on the ego salesman to give them the direction they want and then stick with that choice until they feel they are successful.

The list of aerobic activities is endless and can look overwhelming to all of us. Which is the right one for me? Well, the right one for you is the

one that you will join on a regular basis. The best one is the activity that gives you continuous pleasure and self-esteem. Every activity has benefits for the body, so the activity that you choose *is* the right one for you. Work with what works for you *now*, instead of waiting for climate conditions and divine intervention. Every movement and activity will challenge your heart and lungs; muscles will contract and stretch, and your mind

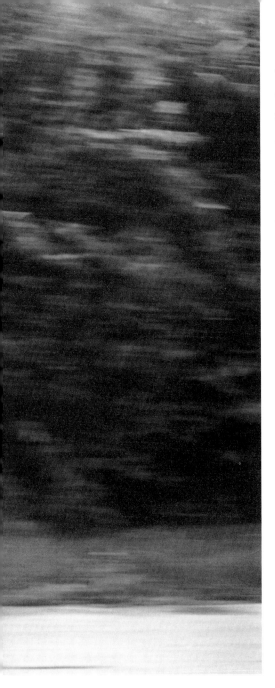

will focus on you and the path ahead of you instead of the responsibilities that life has set down in front of you.

GROUP FITNESS

Group fitness classes have always been a clubhouse for women who have the ability to bounce around endlessly and enjoy the challenge of carefully choreographed routines. Men have been housed in the weight room next to the aerobic room since the early days of the fitness movement, looking in the window occasionally. As a group fitness leader for 10 years, I can tell you that the most difficult part of my job was trying to get men into the room for a class that I know they would benefit from.

In my experience I have learned that men are intimidated by dance exercise classes. They don't want to be made fools of in any arena, and I agree with them. Why should you stand in a room full of strangers and try to hobble around, always on the wrong foot and feeling like a jerk because the pace is so fast that you can't breathe and can never catch up. If you have had dance training in the past, it would be a different scenario. Even if you move well, the slick choreography of some of these classes can be defeating and humiliating.

The best thing to do would be to find a low-impact aerobics class at the beginner level or a step class at the introductory level. The fact is, every person in the group class has been in the same shoes you are in. They all had to make the mistakes and trip over their own feet to learn the foot skills and the directional changes most of that choreography is trying to guide you through. You see, these classes are not out to make you the brunt of any joke. They are an alternative to the automation of a machine that would set you in motion. Your body is the machine in a group class, and the skills that teach you how to carry your body have a direct effect on how you stand and how you move through gravity biomechanically.

Diversity and basics are becoming more of the standard now in many clubs with regard to the group fitness classes. Instead of finding advanced movement classes, with choreography so challenging that the instructor is even having a hard time, look for circuit training or interval training classes that minimize the movements skill and can offer you a successful hour session of aerobic training. Coordination is not a component of this type of class and it can be tailored around your level. You can build up your stamina and work within your strength boundaries without the drill sergeant in your face.

Body-sculpting classes and weighted workouts in the class setting are also a way to break into the classroom or group fitness room. These classes also take a bit of the awkwardness away, helping you feel more comfortable. I always recommend these classes to men so they can get into the room and perform something that they know they can excel at; then they can feel successful and see that the room is inviting and friendly.

Abs classes are also on the rise, and you will find them attended by men and women alike. These classes are popular because they don't require dance skills. Everyone can lie on the floor and everyone is obsessed with having a trimmer waistline. If this is your way in, great; there are many options for you in those classes, so take a risk and try one.

MACHINES

You can find them somewhere on cable television at any given minute of the day, every day of the week. Truly, there have never been so many machines on the market at one time and there will be more to come. They come in and out of fashion like bell bottoms and software. The sellers often rely on the "moment" and the saturation of the product to get you to buy the latest and the greatest, but be aware that the traditional machines are proven and few of the gadgets stay around very long.

Gyms and health clubs have machines lined up like used-car lots or appliance showrooms, in a vast field of blinking lights and on and off switches. The best part is,

you just have to get on and ride it; the machine will take care of you and put you into the movement that it intends to simulate. Most of the time these machines will re-create an activity that you would perform out in the real world, but you don't get anywhere. That is why they are convenient and popular; they are always there with the same result no matter how tired or bored or hassled you are. They are constant and unfeeling. The machine has no responsibility other than to pull, push, lift, or separate you into motion, which will get your body to function at a pace that will promote cardiovascular endurance and burn fat. Some perform better than others, but as with aerobic classes, you have to enjoy the activity in order to show up and do it again and again.

The following activities are singular sports that you can consider for your exercise routine. They require a daily commitment in order to offer you the many benefits, both physical and mental.

I will recommend an equation at the end of each section that will suggest strength-training sets and reps for you to consider. These exercises should be performed three times (days) a week.

Flexibility exercises should be performed every day if possible. This is the most difficult addition to every man's program, but one of the most overlooked and important. Try to get into the habit from the start so it will seem natural to stretch every time you work out.

SWIMMING

Swimming is a highly demanding sport that requires strength and endurance. To look at a swimmer's body, you can see the evidence in square, powerful shoulders, thick lats, and flared backs all the way down to the trim waist and thunderous thighs. The body produces muscle where muscle is needed for the sport of your choice; however, swimming is virtually nonimpact so the stress on your joints is minimal. Many people use swimming as a method of rehabilitation from an injury that occurred in another sport.

Strength training is a vital part of

the competitive swimmer's routine; it helps produce strength and endurance required for propulsion and proper body alignment benefiting the stroke and the kick movements used in swimming.

The best cardiovascular exercises to enhance a swimming program, if a pool is not available at any given time, are step-climbing machines, cross-country ski machines, upper-

body ergometers or a group aerobics class of your preference. Any exercise that helps improve and promote the flexibility and strength of the shoulder and hip joint will help the swimmer maintain full range of motion.

Competitive swimmers compete in short sprints of 50-, 100-, and 200-meter races. Speed and skill are the focus of the contest, but these men must train to gain strength, aer-

obic and anaerobic fitness and flexibility, just like the rest of us.

Basic Training exercises to enhance swimming skills and complement your program: Strength (1–3 sets/12 reps each set)—chest flye, tricep dip, bicep curl, squats, crunches, reverse flye, one-arm row, back flex (1 set only). Flexibility—back-shoulder stretch, chest stretch, half-moon, yoga lunge, neck reliever.

Estimated calories burned in a 30-minute session at moderate intensity = 250. (Est. based on 150-pound man.)

WALKING

Walking is something you do every day without effort or focus. That is just how simple walking can be as a component of your fitness routine and program. If you are just getting started and have a hard time deciding which activity to join, try walking. It will get you going and you will find yourself involved in a program before you know it.

Set a path or a map for your walk and execute your stride just as you would if you were performing any other exercise that requires focus and attention. Keep your shoulders lifted and your midsection tight; this will ensure correct posture at all times. Use your arms to increase the intensity by intentionally pressing and pulling them back and forth, instead of just letting them swing at your sides. This motion will also help you to focus on the walk as an exercise instead of as a chance to cruise around. Your stride will also regulate your speed. If you use a normal walking stride, without stopping and starting, you should be walking about 3.5 miles per hour. This type of stride is good and will create results in someone new to exercise; however, the conditioned may find this pace a waste of time. Walking with a longer stride doesn't necessarily mean you will move faster and reap better benefits; shorter steps at a quicker pace will make you travel faster and help you avoid the overrotation of the hip. Move through the heel, ball, and toe of the entire foot as you walk to keep your form.

To change the action in your hips and ultimately cause your legs to rethink, do the tightrope walk. Imagine a line on your path, road, or sidewalk and walk the line one foot in front of the next. See if you can focus on

that and walk without falling off the line. It will help vary your attention and force your legs and feet to adapt to the new technique.

Walking utilizes the legs (front and back) as well as the upper body and core for posture and support. Strength in the leg as well as the upper body is important to ensure that you are carrying your body instead of just letting it ride on your legs.

Basic Training exercises to enhance walking skills and complement your program: Strength (1–3 sets/12 reps each set)—push-up, tricep extensions, isolated bicep curl, crunch with towel, dead lift, one-arm row, leg extensions, hamstring curl. Flexibility—hip flexor stretch, calf stretch, lower-back stretch.

Estimated calories burned in a 30-minute session with hills = 200.

RUNNING

Running, as research points out, is the most effective method of burning fat when performed correctly, approached with a smart program, and executed with perfect form.

Running has as many positive benefits as it does negative by-products. Because running is considered a high-impact activity, the risk of injury is greater than in cycling or swimming, both of which are considered nonimpact. Impact is just as it sounds: the speed with which the foot meets the ground or the distance of the foot from the ground

will determine the level of impact. Jogging will keep your feet closer to the ground, where an all-out run will probably lift your feet much higher off the ground, resulting in greater impact to the ankle, knee, and hip joints. Every beginner should consider walking first to perfect technique before advancing to running. Also, running in a controlled environment—on a treadmill, for example—will give you the op-

portunity to train and build your stamina for the great outdoors.

Like walking, running is cheap. All you need is a good pair of shoes with support for your arches and ankles and cushioning to absorb the impact of the road. This activity will create changes in your lower body and your abdominals. By stripping your body of fat, you will see your musculature defined and visible. Other activities to enhance your running program would be cycling, rowing, water jogging, jumping rope, and strength training. Always practice good posture and focus ahead of you. It will keep your upper body positioned and keep you aware of the path ahead. Obstacles in your way—curbs and pot holes and unlevel paths—can be hazardous, so be aware of everything. This also keeps you present in the exercise.

Running can even be used along with walking as an interval training tool, another way to feel how running challenges the body. Start by walking two minutes and then run for two minutes. You can decide how long a period of time is right for the switch, and be aware of the amount of time it takes for your heart rate to adjust to the slower pace. Then, using your own perception, spend less time walking and more time running. Soon you will be running the entire session and enjoying what millions of people have been doing for years.

Basic Training exercises to enhance running skills and complement your program: Strength (1–3 sets/12 reps each)—push-up, tricep extensions, bicep curl, crunch with towel, squats. Flexibility—hip-flexor stretch, calf stretch, lower-back stretch, inner-thigh stretch.

Estimated calories burned in a 30-minute session at moderate intensity = 375.

CYCLING

Cycling is a sport that moves and is easy to understand. You get on the bike and go. Many of us have the skill of riding a bike from childhood and for that reason, cycling is great. Not only do you get the results and the rewards of training but you get to remember a fun time in your life, fond friends, or even the bike itself. Today, bikes are more complex and engineered for all types of riding: mountain, urban, and distance. Equipment for this sport has become a billion-dollar industry, and laws in some states require that helmets be worn at all times. Some bikes even require clips on your shoes for a specially designed pedal. If you are stopping and starting during your ride, I would suggest that a traditional pedal will give you more options.

Many runners will cross train with cycling, and ex-runners enjoy the training benefits because of the impact level being reduced from their previous activity. Cycling also covers a lot of territory; you really get to use the environment and enjoy the outdoors as a focal point, depending on the terrain. Flats require speed and rhythm where hills require strength and determination. The area where you live will help you determine whether to buy a road bike or a mountain bike.

Get used to the way the bike works and understand all the gears as well as the maintenance of your bike. You want the bike to work optimally so that you can be assured of the best workout, without running the risk of an accident. Posture and form are critical with cycling, as with all activities. The stress to the lower back is evident just by looking at someone on a bike. Always keep your abs tight, allowing them to support the spine in this position. Your elbows should be relaxed, and focus your eyes in front of you.

The revolution of the pedals will determine your speed. Get comfortable with your pace or ride with a friend. Try to develop a rhythm with the revolutions and develop a cadence, like a drummer setting the tone. This type of mental training helps on long, flat surfaces to break up the time or the climb, where keeping up with the rhythm will assist you when you start to fatigue. Pedal with a smooth motion and break slowly as well. If you are an urban rider, be aware of pedestrians and obstacles in your path. Don't be a jerk; have regard for everyone who is trying to enjoy the outdoors. City dwellers have so little of the environment anyway, share your joy of it.

Cycling strengthens the quadriceps, hamstrings, buttocks muscles, and calves. The lower back and the shoulders are also affected, as are the abdominals. Keep in mind that the heart and lungs are being taxed. It's a good idea to monitor your heart rate in the beginning. Use the talk test to determine how hard you are working.

Using a stationary bike is a smart way to train when the climate doesn't allow you to get outside. Spinning classes, which at the present time are all the rage, simulate an outdoor experience and are considered by many real cyclists to be better than a traditional stationary bike. A spinning bike has a flywheel that creates resistance similar to a steep hill. You have control over how hard you have to work and the speed of each revolution of the pedals.

Basic Training exercises to enhance cycling skills and complement your program: Strength (1–3 sets/12 reps each)—decline push-up, tricep dips, bicep curl, crunch, standing row, squat, back flex (1 set/10 reps). Flexibility—chest stretch, hip-flexor stretch, hamstring stretch, lower-back stretch, inner-thigh stretch.

Estimated calories burned in a 30-minute session at moderate intensity = 350.

BLADING

Blading or in-line skating is a popular hobby and an effective exercise activity. This is where the idea that exercise can be fun can be taken literally. You can blade almost anywhere these days, in a park, along the waterways, in a parking lot (sometimes the best surface of all), or on a rink designed specifically for blades. Wherever you have the space and the skill, get out there and play. Blading is always fun for me. When you get out there for a long period of time, or if you use your blades as a form of transportation, you always meet other blade enthusiasts.

Blading is similar to roller skating and ice skating. You have the option to turn and curve and spin, even race. Because of these options, the chance for an accident is high. Before you decide to get on a pair of blades, gear up with all the apparatus: helmet, elbow pads, knee pads, and wrist guards. If you are just learning, set aside your fashion sense and your ego and learn the smart way to blade. Have someone take you through the motions of stopping and falling. Yes, there is a proper way to fall. If you feel the fall happening, try not to freeze up and put your arms out. Most times the arm will lock and your body will become stiff, like a plank. If you allow the fall to happen, you will roll into the fall and most likely just get a scratch. If your wrist or elbow locks out, the chances of an injury are greater. Blading requires a lot of balance and concentration on form and technique. Your knees should remain soft; a slight lean forward will help you balance.

Stopping requires practice and flexibility in the hamstrings. Stretching your leg forward (the one with the break), then lifting the toes toward you like a hamstring stretch, will press the break to the ground. Try to stop gradually instead of coming to a dead stop. You will most likely fall if you attempt this type of stop, or drag one foot behind you with the front wheel scraping the ground to slow you down and eventually stop.

This activity will strengthen your lower body, including your inner-thigh muscles and your abdominals. You will recruit several muscle groups to help you skate even though you won't know it, but a day or two after

GOLF

Golf has a long history of being a gentleman's sport, and I would be in a heap of trouble with my father if I wrote a book about fitness, with suggestions about sports and activities, and made no mention of golf. Golf has made its way into popular culture and is less for the social elite than it was years ago. It always seemed to be a sport for fat old men or for those who retired to Florida for the winter season. Well, along came a young man by the name of Tiger Woods and changed the sport for the future. In my opinion, he has singlehandedly brought the attention of the world to this sport and has made us look at golf as important and challenging.

Golf is very Zen and challenges the mind of the player. It combines the strategies of chess with the precision of soccer, and the patience of fishing with the competitive skills of archery.

The swing is the foundation of the game. You must develop a strong trunk (torso) and build strength in the middle of your body in order to play the game well. Strength training can enhance the rotary movements of the shoulders as well as the arms and legs, and promoting strength in the abs will prevent lower-back problems. Flexibility is very important to the success of the game, and success is what makes this game fun.

Because this sport doesn't have the intensity of the others mentioned in this chapter, the number of calories burned will be similar to walking. If you think that golf is aerobic while you are riding in the cart, you are mistaken. Every man can benefit from the walk around the golf course. Carrying the clubs will make the workout harder, but a pull cart is okay.

This sport will affect the legs and the shoulders, primarily the back shoulder and the rotators. The rotator cuff may need some conditioning exercises which you will find in the rehab section of the Fundamentals. Equipment requires clubs, of course; shoes should have cleats; and the all-important glove will help to stabilize the club in your hand. Driving ranges are set up for everyone to get some practice, but the course is out there for you to enjoy.

your first time you will never forget the muscles you found out you had. Alternative training for this sport might be running, swimming, or basketball, the first two concentrating on rhythm and the third on explosive bursts to build powerful legs.

Basic Training exercises to enhance blading skills and complement your program: Strength (1–3 sets/12 reps each)—squat, incline push-up, tricep extensions, bicep curls, oblique crunch, dead lift, back flex (1 set/10 reps). Flexibility—hamstring stretch, chest stretch, hip-flexor stretch, lower-back stretch, inner-thigh stretch, half-moon.

Estimated calories burned in a 30-minute session at moderate intensity = 300.

Basic Training exercises to enhance golf skills and complement your program: Strength (1–3 sets/12 reps each)—push-up, tricep extensions, isolated bicep curls, reverse crunch, dead lift, prone leg raises, cross-leg kickbacks. Flexibility— hamstring stretch, chest stretch, hip-flexor stretch, lower-back stretch, back-shoulder stretch, half-moon.

Estimated calories burned in a 30-minute session at moderate intensity = 197.

SKIING

Skiing has three variations: downhill, cross-country, and water, all of which I love. The only problem is getting the opportunity to ski because each type is so seasonal. Skiing requires equipment, snow/water or a machine, money, and balance. Not necessarily in that order. Snow-skiing and water-skiing are not really suitable for a regular fitness regimen, but cross-country skiing offers a total body workout that has been duplicated by several types of cardiovascular machines on the market.

Classical cross-country skiing provides you with the basic technique that will move you forward in tracks. Using the arms and legs at the same time places great physiological demands on the cardiorespiratory system, more than any other sport. These skiers possess the aerobic endurance for extended periods of time in addition to the anaerobic ca-

pacity for climbing hills and uneven terrain.

The upper body and the lower body have to work in partnership in order to create a smooth and balanced stride. It is similar to running on snow or gliding on water. I have even seen a water version of this activity. By gliding through the snow in a rhythmic pace, and by the exertion of the muscle systems to pull

you through gravity, this exercise is ideal. The impact on the joints is minimal and the learning curve varies with the environment. Indoors the activity can be produced on a machine; outdoors the activity takes on a completely different appeal.

The lower body and upper body require strength and flexibility to perform at optimal levels. Training techniques that will enhance this sport should be activities that utilize the same range of motion and speed. Swimming and deep-water running would be great cross-training exercises as well as weight training.

Basic Training exercises to enhance skiing skills and complement your program: Strength (1–3 sets/12 reps each)—push-up, tricep extensions, isolated bicep curls, reverse crunch, dead lift, prone leg raises, cross-leg kickbacks. Flexibility—hamstring stretch, chest stretch, hip-flexor stretch, lower-back stretch, back-shoulder stretch, half-moon.

Estimated calories burned in a 30-minute session at moderate intensity = 300.

ROWING

Rowing is an endurance builder for both the cardiorespiratory system and the muscular system. When I think of rowing I think of a crew paddling on the Potomac River in Washington, a kayak on the Colorado River, or a rowboat in Central Park. During the spring and fall I venture up to Central Park and get into a rowboat and paddle around the lake for an hour or so. It looks good, but I tell you it is a workout.

Just look at the upper body of any crew member or swimmer during the next Olympics and tell me you don't wish to possess such a balanced body. I think that I envy crew members and swimmers most for their balance and physique: powerful legs, strong upper back and shoulders, amazing arms, and a narrow torso. This body type doesn't just happen, it is trained to get that way.

Rowing can be used as a way to warm up for any activity or weight-training session. It supplies the body with blood and lubricates the joints, preparing the body for what is in store. The demand on the legs, shoulders, and arms is very high, so to build these area requires strength training and cross training with step climbing, cross-country ski machines, aerobics classes, and polymetric activities.

A good rowing machine would be one that has a handle attached to a flye wheel; the wheel creates the resistance for the back and shoulders. The gliding seat will cause the legs to bend as you press your body back and forth. The repetition will elevate the heart rate and challenge your entire body.

Basic Training exercises to enhance rowing skills and complement your program: Strength (1–3 sets/12 reps each)—push-up, tricep dips, bicep curls, crunch, squats. Flexibility—hamstring stretch, chest stretch, hip-flexor stretch, lower-back stretch, back-shoulder stretch, half-moon.

Estimated calories burned in a 30-minute session at moderate intensity = 220.

SURFING

This doesn't seem like a sport that would be considered for a fitness routine, but the benefits surfing can create are unique to the sport itself. Surfing requires the participant to meditate and concentrate on the flow of the ocean, to work the upper body by stroking through the water,

to get out to the waves and to balance the legs and lower body to stand
and ride the wave into shore. The
surfer has a respect for the tide and
for the power of the water that a
golfer has for the speed of the green,

a skier has for the powder, and a runner has for the track.

The by-product surfers benefit
from is a square back and strong
shoulders, meaty lats and strong legs.
Surfers hold an isometric contraction

as they stand on the board and then
are required to paddle out to the
waves again, using only their arm
strength and power.

In order to maintain strength for
this sport, rowing machines, cross-

country ski machines, and swimming would be excellent cross-training activities.

Basic Training exercises to enhance surfing skills and complement your program: Strength (1–3 sets/12 reps each)—push-up, tricep dips, bicep curls, crunch, squats. Flexibility—hamstring stretch, chest stretch, hip-flexor stretch, lower-back stretch, back-shoulder stretch, half-moon.

STAIR CLIMBING

There are many benefits to exercising on stair-climbing machines: calorie consumption, strengthening the leg muscles, continuous low-impact movement, and the all-important conditioning aspect for the heart and lungs. There are a variety of step machines with the price points to match. Most of them are good and will provide you with a great workout.

However, the sport doesn't have to be confined to the house. Stair climbing has come out and has found its way into the fitness arena by using the stairs that are provided in the urban environment or in the structure of a building or house. Try not to allow yourself to excuse the possibility of step aerobic conditioning just because you don't have a step machine. There are many forms of stairs out there, you just have to find them. A perfect example of this is in Santa Monica, California, where the famous "steps"—several flights of stairs in a public park—are a virtual playland for the men and women in Los Angeles who climb and descend them for the benefits of cardio training.

If you don't live in Los Angeles, don't rule this out as an option. Use any steps that are available to you. You can use them to run up in quick races with yourself and then walk slowly down them; you can climb them casually or take three steps at a time. The action of the climb uses all the muscles of the leg, including the buttocks as you go upward. You should note that the impact on your knees happens only as you descend any step. Your body weight almost doubles, not because of any meal you have eaten previous to your workout but because gravity combined with the lowering of your own body puts an enormous amount of weight (your body weight times two) on your knee joints. Your knees act as shock-absorbing joints that stop you as you go down a staircase. If you feel discomfort in the knees as you descend a flight of stairs, slow down or use an elevator if one is available. In a park or a staircase at your house, go slowly on the way down and climb naturally through the heel of the foot all the way through the leg. This type of slow and quick motion is similar to interval training. The number of flights of steps will determine the time periods of action and rest (up and down).

Chart a course—the stairs in your house, your apartment building, the office, or a park—and climb. I have mentioned this option before in this book and have seen many of my clients get solid results from this easy-to-adapt routine.

TEAM SPORTS

Play isn't a concept that adults respond to easily after a certain age. We gave up the part of ourselves that was fearless and spontaneous in order to become reliable and responsible adults; and we let go of a special part of our character that made us fun to be around. As children, play was an instinctual part of us; it brought out our creative side, made us work with others as a team and exercised our imagination. We took greater risks at play and developed skills we never knew we possessed. As we grew, organized sports and recreation became a part of us, even if we didn't like them. Gym classes were a requirement and an introduction to the rules and regulations of sports and team play. These activities required a spirit that we lost as adults and must try to nurture once again. The whimsy of play for an adult can result in getting the best out of life.

Think of how it was when you were a boy and how the curiosity of the simplest of things seemed to completely absorb your thinking. I know that life was less complicated then, but just remembering then may help you now with "playing." In sessions with many of my clients, I ask them to "play the game," and what I mean

and punished, but like a kid who will dive right in and get the thrill he knows exists in the action.

WHY PLAY?

• Any sport or game that requires you to move, even moderately, is physically beneficial. The by-product of having a good time is getting fit.

• Try a number of different activities so that your arms and legs move in unfamiliar ranges of motion. Trying different things will prevent injury by using different muscles and will keep you from getting bored.

• You will get in touch with your body without even thinking about it. By putting yourself into an activity, your body responds simply because it has to in order to keep in motion or from falling down. You will also become more aware of where your limbs are in time and in space and in relation to each other.

• Playing is also a problem-solving process. Each game has new challenges and consequences, and by playing along, your brain has to work quickly to get ahead or to win.

• Your sensory system will increase your efficiency at other sports and activities, whether skateboarding and windsurfing, or gardening and cleaning the garage.

• Trying something new and successfully getting through the learning curve builds character and confidence. This type of play attitude will build your self-esteem and help you deal with life in general. It will also help you to understand that simple yet very effective phrase, "It's

is to give up all the facades and humiliation and dive in with that same fearlessness we enjoyed as kids, so that you can realize the possibilities that every activity holds for you.

People tell me that I attack life with enthusiasm, which I do, and I approach life with the same wide-eyed curiosity I had as a boy. I find that people respond to the energy I project. Which would be better, to have a whiny, tired, and negative person around you, or someone who looks at life with optimism and positive energy? I'll take the latter, thank you very much. And this is how I look at activities also. Not like I'm being strapped in

not whether you won or lost, it's how you played the game."

• Playing outside provides an opportunity to enjoy the world; it will connect you to the environment and douse you with fresh air and sunlight. This can also be very therapeutic in helping you forget the problems that lurk in the office and allow you to relax and rekindle that boy spirit.

"PLAY THE GAME"

FOOTBALL

Football demands the ability to block, run, jump, and defend as a member of a team. This sport has the most contact, because even if you are not carrying the ball, someone is either blocking you away from the carrier or defending the carrier trying to pass you. This game, when played among friends, should remain friendly. Remember the rules of play and stick to them. If it is touch football, then try not to tackle, no matter how intense the game. Be a sport.

A friendly game of football, in the park or at the beach, is really fun, and even just passing the ball keeps you moving. The operative word here and throughout this book is *moving*. In order to reap the benefits of any activity, you have to move. The effect on your heart and lungs will follow, and you will have had a great time getting there.

Total body strength is necessary for a good football player in order to run for the touchdown, catch the man holding the ball, and to prevent injuries, especially those that happen close to the end of the game when fatigue sets in. Blocking and tackling hold their share of injury risks, so the better the condition you are in, the lower the risk of injury. By maintaining your fitness level you will also recuperate from an injury much quicker than someone less fit. The strength of the muscle has a direct influence on the ability and length of your recovery from an injury, no matter how slight.

Serious football should be left to the professionals, but a sandlot game here and there is tons of fun and a great workout at the same time. Make sure you have equipment appropriate to the level of intensity at which you are playing. The best advice is to wear a cup athletic supporter. If you have ever been hit in the groin by a football you will understand the reason I mention it. Also, the contact aspect of this game sometimes leads to an unfortunate punch in the groin area.

Basic Training exercises to enhance football skills and complement your program: Strength—military press, push-ups, lateral raises, flyes, bicep curls, tricep dips, lunges, kickbacks, leg extensions, crossovers, reverse crunches. Flexibility—quad-flexor stretch, lower-back stretch, back-shoulder stretch, hamstring stretch, chest stretch, inner-thigh stretch, neck reliever.

Estimated calories burned in a 30-minute game at moderate intensity = 250.

BASKETBALL

This sport is highly aerobic and it's a fat burner. When was the last time you saw a fat basketball player? Basketball requires you to be fast, stop on a dime, jump as high as you can, change direction in a flash, and run the length of the court at any given minute. The pace is quick and the demands on your energy are great. This sport requires a few players to make it a game, but even on your own the game can be challenging. I have a hard enough time trying to get the ball in the hoop, let alone dribbling it. Shooting hoops by yourself is an activity that includes all the components of a good aerobic workout, because when the ball lands on the ground you have to recover it and then try again, and this repetition will give you a great workout. Then to get into a game with a few guys will be better, then a league, then the NBA!

Conditioning is important in every activity, to ensure that technique is respected and applied, and to prevent injuries when you participate in any sport. Basketball is high-level activity, and if you haven't played in years, you should prepare for it. The risk is your own, but

training as well, so pick up a ball and start.

Basic Training exercises to enhance basketball skills and complement your program: Strength—military press, lateral raises, flyes, bicep curls, tricep dips, lunges, kickbacks, leg extensions, crossovers, reverse crunches. Flexibility—hip-flexor stretch, lower-back stretch, back-shoulder stretch, hamstring stretch, chest stretch, inner-thigh stretch, neck reliever.

Estimated calories burned in a 30-minute game at moderate intensity = 280.

TENNIS

Tennis is a demanding game that requires physical conditioning and mental focus. To see a tennis player who is strong and agile, who has the ability to run with speed and control, to hit the ball with power and precision, is simply beautiful. Like a trained dancer or a skilled sensei, the tennis player combines tremendous skills in one sport. Look at the required components of a good tennis player: balance, mental attitude and focus, speed, flexibility, agility, endurance, coordination, strength. Looking at that list will indicate that tennis isn't the gentile sport so many make it out to be. In the recent years we have seen tennis become a bad boy sport with the likes of John McEnroe and (my personal favorite) Andre Agassi. These men brought into tennis an attitude that made us sit up and take notice.

you will play better and feel better a couple of days after if you are in shape than you will if you have been sitting there for a few years and one day decide to get out and play a few games. How often has that happened to you? Really?

Basketball stars of today seem bigger, more muscular than they ever have. Strength will play a factor in every sport that requires speed and powerful jumps. Due to the fact that the game keeps moving, the aerobic benefits are high, and to promote muscle strength, heavier weight and lower reps equations should be applied for gains and for maintenance.

There are many places to play basketball, at the local playground, gymnasiums at the Y, in health clubs, or even in front of your garage. Excuses are only a way out; you can always find something to do. Dribbling a ball is considered

Because the sport is so driven by speed and quick movement, tennis is not the sport for the weight lifter or for someone who wants a muscular build. The need to move like a gazelle is vital and the power and explosive movements needed are not the type that a musclebound athlete can produce. For incorrectly trained players, tennis can produce many injuries. Lateral-movement drills are important due to the fact that this sport requires you to run from side to side and upward and back. This is a game of controlled force and precise technique.

Training the muscle systems for endurance means you should increase the number of repetitions over the amount of weight used when you are training. Training the strength of the core of the body (abdominals) is also key because your body is moving continuously, and supporting the middle of the body will decrease the risk of injury to your back. Lower-back stress is a common complaint among tennis players, so take the advice I am giving you here and now and make sure you strengthen your abdominal muscles for general good health and fitness and the rest of your activities will only be better.

Other activities that will complement your game include jumping rope, running and sprinting, circuit training, as well as specific hop drills, jumping from one place to the next either front to back or side to side. Hands require specific training as well to promote a stronger grip and wrist strength. Pressing your fingers together with fully extended open hands will stretch the hands. Using a hand grip clip, similar to the clip you would use with a barbell to hold the plates on the bar, will strengthen the fingers as you repeatedly grip the clip. Squeezing a tennis ball or a softer type of ball will also strengthen the hand and condition the forearm.

Many tennis players also suffer from rotator-cuff discomfort or injuries, so make sure you strengthen and stretch the shoulders enough to counterbalance the continuous demands you place on the shoulders with each swipe at the ball. The repeated volleying of the ball forces the arm to move quickly and with great force, so the muscle needs to be in good condition at all times. If you have an injury, rest is the best advice I can give you.

Basic Training exercises to enhance tennis skills and complement your program: Strength—bent-over row, front raises, lateral raises, flyes, isolated bicep curl, revere curls, lunge, hamstring curl, leg extensions, crossovers, reverse crunch. Flexibility—hip-flexor stretch, lower-back stretch, back-shoulder stretch, hamstring stretch, chest stretch, inner-thigh stretch.

Estimated calories burned in a 30-minute game = 230 singles / 100 doubles.

MARTIAL ARTS

There are many forms of martial arts—karate, kung fu, Tae Kwon Do, aikido, judo, and Tai Chi, to name a few. Each requires a highly developed level of fitness with emphasis on power, flexibility, and speed. As in wrestling, the upper body requires strength in the arms, chest, and upper back for controlled and sudden movement skills such as grabbing, punching, pushing, and throwing. The lower body maintains stance, direction, and balance, so strength in the lower body is vital. Flexibility is critical with all of the martial arts. High kicking and sweeps require the hip flexors to act like an elastic band, and strength is needed in the lower back, upper leg, and buttocks to assist in all of those key movements.

The martial arts require a great deal of mental focus and clarity. This aspect of the sport causes many men to turn away; it gets too personal. The intimacy of the sport helps you to unlock your true potential and helps you to realize that you are a powerful and vital being in the universe. When men hear this type of language they generally turn off, lower the volume, or brain freeze. This type of training goes too deep for some, but allows those who accept and practice these arts a tranquil self-awareness that so many men wish they could understand.

Training for the martial arts can include aerobic conditioning, cross-country ski machines, and rowing machines. Yoga is a wonderful complement to the martial arts because it increases flexibility and helps the participant concentrate on breathing technique and balance.

Basic Training exercises to enhance martial art skills and complement your program: Strength—military

press, front raises, upright row, one-arm row, reverse laterals, push-ups, incline push-up, tricep extension, balanced lunge, squats, leg extensions, crunches (1 set of 75), reverse crunches (2 sets of 20), fishhooks (2 sets of 25 each side). Flexibility—hip-flexor stretch, lower-back stretch, back-shoulder stretch, chest stretch, hamstring stretch, inner-thigh stretch.

Estimated calories burned in a 30-minute match at moderate intensity = 300.

VOLLEYBALL

Volleyball can be played at the beach, in a park, or, now, in YMCAs and fitness clubs across the country. This is one of those team sports that will remind you of your youth or at least remind you of my youth. Picking up a ball with some bounce and hitting it back and forth is usually the way the game starts, and then you can get into some type of formula. I played that way until years later someone told me there were rules and regulations that we had to adhere to. All I knew was that it was fun, and it always made me want to jump into the water to cool off. Therefore, the activity was aero-bic enough to get us sweating, quick enough to challenge the power in our legs, and with the pace to challenge our coordination. Sounds to me like the activity had all the components of exercise, but the fun quotient seemed higher than formal exercise.

Volleyball is played with four (two on a team), eight (four on a team), or twelve (six on a team) people on each squad. The number of people on the teams will determine the intensity level by giving each player a definite role. As the teams get bigger, the more downtime you have to rest, but playing two on two is very active and requires you to be

involved at all times. In any case, keep the game fun and upbeat; use sportsmanship and teamwork.

Skills such as spiking, setting, and the bump involve the upper-body muscle groups, which take quite a bruising. Strong and flexible shoulders require the arms to extend above the head repeatedly. The power of your arms will assist in the spike, and explosive leg muscles will get you above the net for the all-important spike.

Indoor volleyball will require some equipment for safety; namely, knee pads and elbow pads. The floor surface has no conscience and is very different from the sand at the beach and the grass in the park, so protect the important joints that you will need for the rest of your life. Don't compromise your judgment for a killer game without protection.

Continuous jumping skills are required if you want to get serious about volleyball. Jumping rope is a great tool for building up the endurance in your legs for competitive play. To maintain your fitness level and complement your volleyball participation, running on a treadmill, circuit training, and sprinting on foot or on a cycle will keep your anaerobic system energized.

Basic Training exercises to enhance volleyball skills and complement your program: Strength—military press, front raises, one-arm row, reverse laterals, decline push-up, tricep extension, balanced lunge, squats, leg extensions, crunches with towel. Flexibility—hip-flexor stretch, lower-back stretch, back-shoulder stretch, hamstring stretch.

Estimated calories burned in a 30-minute game at moderate intensity = 200.

WRESTLING

To include wrestling in this chapter may seem odd to you, but to understand the components of this sport is to understand and practice many of the fundamentals of movement and strength. Dynamic movements such as jumping, rolling, running, and crawling are combined with movements that are performed in place such as lifting, pushing, bending, and twisting. All of these movements, along with isometric skills such as gripping and releasing, require a

high level of muscle conditioning, especially leg and arm strength. This is a grueling sport, requiring endurance, flexibility, and agility. Additional skills depend on the strength of the upper body, the biceps, forearms, and mid-back for pulling and pushing.

This sport is not as accessible to the average exercise enthusiast, but the benefits can be the same. You challenge both your strength and cardiovascular systems at the same time. This sport requires additional training that can benefit every sportsman. Finding a wrestling program may be difficult, so check your local YMCA or local gymnasium for availability.

The one-on-one approach also has its own appeal, because of the fact that you are really testing your own physical strength and endurance every time you participate. Wrestling is very similar to self-defense due to the fact that you are extremely focused and challenged by your opponent. Your skill level will determine the outcome of the match, and the opponent should be respected. This sport requires mental focus, strategic planning, and keen direction or coaching. Because of the physical nature of the sport, many men may turn away from it, but when performed at its best this sport is like a dance, a perfect layup, a line drive, a home run.

Basic Training exercises to enhance wrestling skills and complement your program: Strength—military press, front raises, upright row, one-arm row, reverse laterals, push-ups, incline push-up, tricep extension, balanced lunge, squats, leg extensions, crunches (1 set of 75), reverse crunches (2 sets of 20). Flexibility—hip-flexor stretch, lower-back stretch, back-shoulder stretch, hamstring stretch, inner-thigh stretch.

Estimated calories burned in a 30-minute match at moderate intensity = 320.

BOXING

Boxing has made its way out of the ring and into the mainstream. It isn't just for the guys in the training gyms that we have seen in movies like *Rocky;* it's now in health clubs and group exercise classes. Set to music, this type of

training gives you a great understanding and respect for the boxer and the dance that they perform in each match.

Boxing is highly aerobic because of the feet; they never stop moving and neither does the body attached. Internalizing the rhythm of music is a secret key the boxer uses and now the secret is being shared with the masses. The boxer utilizes jabs and hooks in a succession of repetitions like a well-choreographed dance routine so that when he needs to throw a group of punches at his opponent, it will come naturally. In the heat of a match, you have to rely on memory, because having the crap beat out of you, your body must respond with all the ammunition it has.

Boxing has changed in the past few years with the strength factor increasing the power punch. Using heavier weight has given boxers today a stronger, more muscular body; they reduce the amount of repetitions so as to add bulk to the body, like the awesome Evander Holyfield. Endurance is gained with polymetrics and jumping rope as it was traditionally done in the past.

The midsection of the boxer has to be in top condition in order to take all those punches, so training the abdominal muscles would seem unreal to the normal person; however, the jabs and the punching affect the abs more than you think they do. Speed bags and shadow boxing are great techniques for the amateur, and believe me, if you give half of the effort a boxer puts out, you will feel the work in your abs for days.

Basic Training exercises to enhance boxing skills and complement your program: Strength—front raises, lateral raises, flyes, dead lift, bicep curl, reverse curls, lunge, squats, crunches, reverse crunch, fishhook. Flexibility—hip-flexor stretch, neck reliever, low-back stretch, back-shoulder stretch, front-shoulder stretch, hamstring stretch, chest stretch, inner-thigh stretch.

Estimated calories burned in a 30-minute session at moderate intensity = 280.

WEEKEND WARRIORS

I love the weekend warrior. The man who packs in all of his weekly activity into the two days a week. Tennis in the morning, followed by a brisk run, then lunch and a walk in the park, possibly blading and then bowling with friends and an IV bag with a drip of liquid ibuprofen until he has to go to work on Monday morning. Or the guy who chauffeurs the kids, and then participates in everything they egg him on to do, forgetting that they are 25 years younger than he is and ever was. I really admire the weekend warrior, because he does possess the right attitude; he just needs to spread things out a little.

Everything that he does in those two days can be done all week long. Trying to fit it into the right day of the week and find the right training partner are the more difficult part. The weekend also gives you the opportunity to do things that are more extreme in nature; things you never imagined you could or would do. This type of man is adventuresome, and I admire him for his ability and his "play" attitude. Just what I have been talking about, but a little beyond.

Higher risk activities are for those men who have that edge—for the fearless, the adventurers, the insured: rock wall climbing, bungee jumpers, motor-cross riders, sky divers, hang gliders, jet skiers, and whitewater riders are a few. Their heart rate jumps just because of the excitement; they are burning fat just sitting there. Kidding aside, all of these sports and activities have a high level of difficulty, and I would advise you to learn about them and have someone acquaint you with whatever is necessary to succeed as well with the risks involved.

Here are a few weekend warrior activities that seem a little more palatable for the average man.

HIKING

When you get out to hike, you are introduced to a new respect for your body and the strength required to climb. This is one reason rock climbing has become so popular, because it will keep those diehard hikers in condition for the seasons they can climb mountains. This sport requires

physical strength and endurance due to the fact that you are constantly climbing or descending. The changes in how much you're pressing your body weight through gravity play a role in how hard your muscle systems are working.

Lower-body strength is crucial for climbing steep passes and for lowering your body weight as you descend hills and changing levels. High steps and ravines require you to jump and lift, so the leg muscles need to be conditioned before you attack the mountain or hills. If you attempt to hit the hills without any preparation, be aware that you will feel it in your legs for days after you have enjoyed the great outdoors, vowing never to do it again unless your prepare for it.

Basic Training exercises to enhance hiking skills and complement your program: Strength—military press, front raises, one-arm row, reverse laterals, decline push-up, tricep extension, balanced lunge, squats, leg extensions, crunches with towel. Flexibility—hip-flexor stretch, lower-back stretch, back-shoulder stretch, hamstring stretch.

TRIATHLONS

This is the epitome of cross training, the ultimate! Combining swimming, running, and cycling in one sport. Triathletes are highly trained sportsmen with competitive spirits. These men spend a remarkable amount of time training and perfecting skills in three sports instead of one, focusing on form and technique as well as nutrition and lifestyle outside of their sport.

The requirements for this sport are above the norm. It would be more realistic to train for each individual sport first and then combine two; for example, cycling and swimming first. In swimming, train to perfect your stroke and breathing rhythm as well as your endurance. Cycle at intensities that will increase your stamina by climbing gradual inclines or hills and take indoor cycling classes such as spinning. These two sports will complement each other in the beginning and offer better balance to most of your muscle groups.

Then add running into your program by replacing the cycling component for a few weeks. After a four-week period combine the three varieties and see what your distances are. Set goals that are realistic at first so that you are able to achieve the marks you have set and then evaluate your performance. Work on the areas where you feel you need help and continue with your training.

Triathlons range in distance and, depending on the terrain and climate, can be brutal if you are unprepared for the competition. The ultimate is the Ironman, a competition designed to separate the men from the boys. Each year men will compete in Hawaii for the title of Ironman, and the title says it all: These men are made of steel. Their mental focus and stamina as well as their highly trained bodies are the envy of most athletes. Train smart for this sport and pay strict attention to balance and flexibility.

Basic Training exercises to enhance triathlon skills and complement your program: Strength—military press, front raises, one-arm row, reverse laterals, decline push-up, tricep extension, bicep curl, balanced lunge, squats, leg extensions, crunches with towel, crossovers. Flexibility—hip-flexor stretch, lower-back stretch, back-shoulder stretch, hamstring stretch, inner-thigh stretch, half-moon.

PART THREE:

Lifestyle

CHAPTER EIGHT

The Gym Experience

Some people feel right at home at a gym or club. Others find themselves uncomfortable in a place filled with strangers, all of whom seem to know each other, the ropes, and the best parking spots. The success of your individual fitness program depends on your comfort level—how can you enjoy working out in a place where you feel like an outsider? The trick is to make yourself an insider by getting to know the way the club is run, by asserting your right to be treated well, and by entering into the spirit of the place.

JUDGING THE GYM

FRIENDLY PATRONS AND STAFF

There's no end to the ways in which nice people are nicer than not-nice people: Anyone who's been given the cold shoulder in school or who was always the last one chosen for kickball knows what I'm talking about. On your first visit to a gym, check out the staff. Are they welcoming and friendly, or is the person at the reception desk more interested in his magazine than in greeting you? First impressions are lasting because they set the tone of a place for its patrons. And the behavior of the staff may unconsciously reflect the attitude of the management: Is it appreciative of your patronage, or is it bored, indifferent, even hostile? I would never work out in a gym where people didn't treat me with courtesy and respect, no matter how "hot" or trendy a place is sup-

posed to be. And why would I want to spend a week in a club whose members re-create the horrors of junior high school?

A club where people seem friendly and encouraging is definitely a place you want to be. But even at a place that looks as though it will be fun, you need to ask some questions. Do trainers offer advice and helpful suggestions as they walk around? Or do they concentrate on their own clients, ignoring everyone else? Do patrons share equipment, letting each other "work in" and otherwise welcome newcomers? Or do they give the impression of holding court in an old-boys' club? And let's face it, some gyms are definitely "scenes," essentially singles bars or gay bars with weight racks. Are you comfortable in that kind of environment? If so, fine. If not, you should look elsewhere. Before you shell out a hefty membership fee, plan to spend some time at the place, either as a part of an introductory offer—that is, a free workout offered by the management as an incentive to join—or by paying for a day pass, a cheap enough way to find out how you feel about the joint. It all depends on what you want from the gym experience. Some guys work out as part of their fitness program: They're in and they're out and they don't think too much about it. But other men want the social life and camaraderie, the how-you-doin's and conversations that can—and should—come with the territory. Again, it's up to you: business or pleasure? Whatever you decide, be sure to do your homework. Otherwise you could find yourself stuck at a gym you hate, dreading every visit, or, even worse, not going at all. A club membership is a big investment; be sure and make yours count.

JUICE BAR: DOES IT WALK THE WALK?

Some gyms have juice bars, which can range from a Snapple vending machine to a gleaming restaurant where you'd be proud to take your boss to lunch. Whatever your gym offers, use your judgment and ask yourself what you're being served—and asked to pay for. Obviously, if all you've got to choose between is brands of bottled water, you won't have to investigate further. But there are clubs, supposedly dedicated to their clients' health, that offer up salads in deep-fried tortilla bowls. What does that say about the culture of the place? Are they more interested in profit than in your well-being? If so, you may decide to look elsewhere. On the other hand, you could always brown-bag it, bringing your own water and a snack. Just don't get caught up in the corporate ethos of the place if you don't want to.

GYM RATS

This is the sometimes-affectionate term for those individuals who make the club their home, whether through enthusiasm, loneliness, or exceptionally ambitious fitness programs. When we like them, they're fun to be around, almost always mak-

ing helpful suggestions and making us feel that we belong. When we don't like them, they look like driven, obsessive nuts whose focus on their bodies looks crazy. The extreme form of this is exercise addiction, and whether it's because of an underlying eating disorder or some crash body-building course, it's a genuinely dangerous condition. Learn the warning signs, both in others and yourself:

1. trouble sleeping

2. appetite loss

3. extreme weight loss (more than 10 percent of total body weight within six months)

4. loss of focus and concentration

5. intestinal problems—severe or prolonged constipation or diarrhea

174

Commitment and enthusiasm about your health and fitness program are great, but some people have a tendency to go overboard, especially when measuring themselves against others. That's why I suggest that you keep your own goals in your fitness log and that you stick to them. If someone at the club asks you why you're not doing lat pull downs with more weight, answer politely but firmly: This is what you feel comfortable doing. Trying to impress a gym rat with more weight or reps than you can safely handle is not a good way to make friends or get in shape.

I would never suggest that you pass up the opportunity to make friends; after all, more than half the pleasure of the gym experience is sharing your pride and fun with others. But the regulars can make you feel welcome or miserable, depending on whether or not you let them. This is the advice your mother would have given you—whether you wanted it or not. The best way to have a good time is to make friends with your colleagues. If they don't seem friendly, make them friendly. A smile is inexpensive, and a word of encouragement to someone struggling on the treadmill may yield dividends on a day when you feel pushed to the wall. So much of the playground fear we remember from grade school is just that—fear. The buff guys you've been admiring or envying have been doing this for quite a while—and they had to start somewhere, too. On the other hand, you may think you're being the strong, silent type while others see you as aloof, unfriendly—certainly no one they'd even say "hi" to. The message is the oldest one. Treat people with respect and friendliness, and you're likely to get the same treatment right back at you.

ETIQUETTE, OR THE BEAUTIFUL ROOM IS NOT EMPTY

Yes, there is an etiquette to the gym experience, because whenever more than one person shows up, the feelings of others have to be taken into consideration. Also, the gym is a place where guys swing heavy weights around, often without looking. So there's a safety element as well to the dos and don'ts of the club. Unless you time your visits so that the place is empty, at some point you will have to share a piece of equipment or a set of weights with someone else. Remember the playground refrain: Share, share, that's fair. Everyone has heard horror stories of arriving at the gym during peak time and witnessing a fight over the last available StairMaster. The law of the jungle pertains to timed machines: first come, first served. But not so elsewhere: If you're planning on doing three sets on the cable pulleys, and you see someone looking hopefully at the station as you're nearing the end of your first set, don't ignore him. What do you say? You say, "Would you like to work in?" Translation: Yes, I was here first, but I'm doing sets, which require a rest period of a minute or two, so why don't you do one of your sets while I'm doing that . . ." It means that two people can work out on one piece of equipment without either of them losing a minute of quality gym time. The same thing holds for a set of weights, and it's in this spirit of cooperation that gym friendships are made and maintained. The guy you invited to work in with you will almost certainly return the favor when he gets the chance. And in the atmosphere of the gym, you'll be seen as a good guy. Okay? Now you speak the language too.

Some men are—how shall I put this delicately?—heavy sweaters. This is fine for the circulation—it cools you off and keeps you comfortable during a long workout. Unfortunately, what it does to an exercise bench may not be appreciated by the next person. So get into the habit of working out with a towel: Before you sit or lie down on a piece of equipment, drape it with the towel, and when you're finished, give the bench or seat or whatever a swipe with the towel. Your mom would be proud and your fellow gymgoers will appreciate the gesture (not to mention the dry surface).

Let's face it—some days are worse than others. No one can be cheerful and up all the time. Your workout time belongs to *you,* but somehow exercise is more fun when we're not hating everyone else in the room. On any given day you may not feel like discussing the state of the nation or even the latest film, but try to be at least civil, even on April 15. Rather than being solely a he-man, macho venue, the gym is also a place where men

bring their hopes, aspirations, perspirations (keep that towel at the ready), and vulnerabilities. You don't have to be your brother's keeper, but keep his feelings in mind. And someone might just be there for you when you need a kind word or a friendly smile.

IS THE CLUB CLEAN?

The best way to rate a club is in the locker rooms. Look in all the nooks and crannies of the facility and put them to a test. Would you feel comfortable walking around barefoot on the tile? Are the showers clean and odor free? Are the lockers spacious and clean? Is there soap in the dispensers? If towels are part of the amenities, are they clean? Does the steam room resemble a biology project? Out on the gym floor does the floor look clean and well maintained? Are the mats sticky from sweat? Are the machines wiped down? Face it, there are lots of germs that can breed at the gym and for your money you are entitled to a scrupulously clean and well-maintained facility.

Take the time to go through the entire facility and evaluate the space according to your own standard. Be fair and realize that the hour you are there could also determine how clean it is or should be. Some clubs clean all day long, some at night, some in the morning. Ask about it, determine whether its cleanliness schedule coincides with your valuable time.

IS THE STAFF EDUCATED AND CERTIFIED?

It should be important to you that the people who are taking you through classes or weight-training programs have some formal or recognized education about how the body functions. Not only is safety the issue, but if physical progress and positive change are what you are buying, you should get them from an authorized dealer. There are many people who start training with a buddy, perhaps someone from the gym, who seems to know what he is doing. That's what a gym is about, working out in public. But be cautious of any exercises that seem homemade or

invented. What works for some bodies doesn't mean that those same things can work for your body.

Look to the staff for guidance and direction. Staff members of many fitness facilities require their teachers and trainers to be certified by one or more associations that recognize education and professionalism. The most widely recognized associations are ACSM (American College of Sports Medicine), ACE (American Counsel on Exercise), and AFAA (Aerobic and Fitness Association of America). The men and women who take the time and money (and the amount of both would surprise you) to continue their knowledge base are the people you should feel very comfortable taking direction from. They also must be trained for CPR and first aid to keep their certificates, so that assurance is comforting.

WHAT IS THE POLICY ON CANCELING OR FREEZING A MEMBERSHIP?

Everyone has a life and sometimes the events in yours may take you out of town or away from the gym for a period of time. It is important to understand that not all clubs are created equal. Some will permit you to freeze the time on your membership and resume the remaining time upon your return. Make sure that this is stated in the contract or agreement that you sign at the point of purchase. It may seem like a stupid thing to consider, but when you get that three-month gig out of town and find that you've forfeited 90 days of your membership, you've gotten no bargain.

IS THE CLUB CLOSE TO HOME OR WORK?

You should really consider the convenience of working out close to home or work. This is a tactic I use with

clients and friends to help them commit and keep showing up. The location can be an issue if the club you feel is right for you is out of the way. If the atmosphere and the people don't matter and you are the type who just wants to do the work and get on with your day, then location can be very important. Consider how often you are far away and how convenient it will be to get to. Is the gym in your route of daily tasks? Can you drop in before, during, or after work? Is it next door? If the place you choose is less of a hassle to get to, you will go. If you go, you will get fitter. Simple.

WILL THEY LET YOU WORK OUT ONCE FOR FREE?

You should be able to try any club once; even if you must pay, try it. If you don't have to pay and they welcome you to join a gym for a single workout, take them up on the offer. Fitness should not be for some special few; everyone should have the opportunity to get fit. This is just good policy, if you ask me. Good policies demonstrate the regard the club management has toward its members. Well-run gyms understand that service to the client is what the client is paying for. It should be a privilege for them to work for you—don't ever think the opposite.

DO YOU FEEL COMFORTABLE IN THE SPACE AND WITH THE PEOPLE?

You want to be comfortable and motivated by the people around you. These are people you are going to be spending time with, not an hour or so but lots of time. You shouldn't feel intimidated or threatened by any of them. Sometimes the "scene" can get out of hand, and although you may like that at first, the A list might not be as attractive the 679th time. The gym is like a community center or church. You will be attracted to the right place for you.

FASHION RULES

Just as in any public environment, what you wear can be important to some and to others foolish even to think about. Fashion dictates to many and is a part of the reason for this book. Styles come in and out, as do body types. There are many choices and fads we have to keep up with as a culture. The fitness culture is not immune to this. Since the fitness revolution made its way onto the street, fitness has created a fashion all its own. Once only seen in the gym, jogging suits and sweats have become a huge part of the main floor in most clothing stores.

Fashion does dictate, but for the sake of getting fit, comfort and durability are the qualities to look for in your gym outfit. We have talked about shoes and what to look for and how to pack if you're going to the gym, but for the sake of comfort, there are a few things to consider.

Fabric: Cotton is the most comfortable fabric to wear, it breathes and absorbs moisture. You should consider this because you will be sweating, or at least you *should* be sweating. Cotton or cotton blended with polyester will also wash and dry easily. Lycra and suplex are man-made fibers that are very popular with the whole cycling crowd with that leaner tight fit many wear. These fabrics were developed for the sake of the athletic competitor, so you can consider them good for most exercise programs. Personal taste plays an important role here as does ego, because this body-conscious look leaves nothing to the imagination. You will see every ripple and bulge, so if this is your choice, keep in mind the rest of the world will see your bulges as well. If you're fine with that, then go for it.

Keeping your clothes clean is just a given. If you don't wash your clothes, you could develop a skin rash from the perspiration left in the fabric, and the smell could result in losing a few friends. Some of these fabrics I have just mentioned will hold on to an odor if they are not washed regularly; even rinsing won't eliminate the smell of sweat. Drying your clothes on a line or in the dryer will also determine whether or not you can wear them again. Many of the fabrics I have described may shrink in the dryer, so read the label for instructions. Even if you exercise in your home, wash your clothes every couple of workouts.

Everyone has his own personal comfort level; some body temperatures are warmer than others. Depending on your own temperature, decide whether long pants or shorts are for you. The same applies to long-sleeve shirts, T-shirts, and tank tops. Layers of course will keep you warmer and textures will insulate you when necessary.

Color can be very important if you are exercising outside. Light colors reflect sunlight and will keep you cooler than dark colors, which absorb light. Depending on the season and the temperature, choose your clothing wisely.

Layer up in the wintertime; you could always shed a layer if you need to. In the summertime, make sure that you wear lightweight clothing so you won't be overcome with heat. If this happens, find shade and hydrate with water or a sports drink.

CHAPTER NINE

Grooming and Personal Hygiene

Most men don't spend a lot of time or trouble on their skin. The lucky ones will still manage to look pretty good—a question of genetic predisposition. But ignoring problems or insisting on frying yourself in the sun can result in blemished, scarred, or wrinkled skin—or even worse. With just a few minutes of care and precaution a day, you can clean and protect the largest organ of your body—because that's what your skin is.

DAILY REGIME

If you have normal to dry skin, your routine is a simple one: Wash your body and face with a mild, unscented soap, such as Dove, Basis, or Purpose. Before you towel off completely, use an unscented moisturizer—Cetaphil, Neutrogena, and Eucerin Light are all good choices, because they're light and nonsticky. Slather on the stuff while your skin is slightly damp—this will hold the moisture in the skin.

If you follow your shower with a shave, you're all set. Your face is now hydrated, and the moisture will help prepare your skin for your shave. But men who are getting acne for the first time in their twenties might want to reconsider their shaving technique. When you shave, you're scraping off a very thin top layer of skin, and this can leave the skin more susceptible to bacteria. Doctors recommend a bactericidal aftershave (such as witch hazel) and suggest that men prone to ingrown hairs and infections in the beard area should use a rotary shaver,

which lifts the hairs, and shave only in the direction of beard growth. If you prefer a wet shave, consider using disposable razors and tossing them often to avoid bacterial buildup. Whichever you use, follow the direction of beard growth, avoiding as best you can moles or blemishes. After your shave, treat cuts and nicks with a cotton swab dipped in hydrogen peroxide solution. Now you're ready for sunscreen.

Despite what you may have heard or would like to believe, there's no such thing as a safe tan. Use a sunscreen every single day, regardless of the weather, and you'll avoid ultraviolet rays that can penetrate cloud cover and, eventually, your skin, resulting in premature wrinkling, freckles, blotching, and skin cancers. New York City dermatologist Dr. Steven A. Victor advises his patients to use a sunscreen with an SPF (sun protection factor) of at least 15 for their bodies and at least 30 for their faces. If you put it on after your morning shave, you won't have to think about it for the rest of the day—unless you go swimming or snorkeling or any activity that keeps you out in the sun or that makes you work up a sweat. Then you'll have to reapply. You should apply your sunscreen at least 30 minutes before going out into the sun.

Sunscreens work in one of two ways. Physical blocks contain ingredients like titanium dioxide, which serve as an actual barrier to UV rays. Chemical blocks such as cinnamate, oxybenzone, and homosalate absorb the sun's rays, and because it can take up to half an hour for these chemicals to become active on your skin, you should apply your sunscreen 30 minutes before going out into

the sun. A few I like: Neutrogena Moisture SPF 15, Shade SPF 30 Oil-Free Gel, and Shade SPF 45 Lotion. In the early days of sunscreen research, most products contained para-amino benzoic acid (PABA) as their active ingredient. But people who used PABA sunscreen tended to get allergic reactions, and today most labels boast that the product within is "PABA-free," good news for sensitive skin. Sunscreens come in different formulations: Try a cream or lotion for dry to normal skin, or a gel for oily skin. A four-ounce bottle or tube will set you back from five to nine bucks, and there's no single product on the market that can do more to protect your skin against premature aging and sun damage. There is absolutely no excuse for not wearing sunscreen every single day. It's the cheapest, easiest way to protect your skin—the only one you've got—from the ravages of the sun.

CONQUERING ACNE

Acne is actually a complex interaction between hormonal activity, bacterial agents, and sebum, the oil produced by glands under the skin. The tendency to acne is hereditary; if one or both of your parents had acne, chances are that you've developed it as well. Some men endure a brief bout of acne in their teens and are fortunate enough to grow out of it. Others continue to suffer the slings and arrows of outrageous blemishes well into their twenties, thirties, and even forties. The good news is that there are many treatments that work, some available over the counter and some that your doctor has to prescribe. But not every case of acne sends a guy off to his doctor. If you get an occasional zit or cluster of blackheads, a product with 5 or 10 percent benzoyl peroxide should clear things up. But be patient. "Most individuals misuse over-the-counter medications," Victor maintains. "They don't follow the instructions carefully, and they switch from one formula to another too quickly." Dr. Victor suggests that you try a product for at least six weeks before you decide whether or not it's doing any good. For more severe cases of acne—constant pustules and in-

flamed cysts and lesions—you should see your doctor, who will probably begin by prescribing a combination of benzoyl peroxide and a topical antibiotic. Oral antibiotics are often used, and "Tetracycline is a mainstay," Victor notes. The problem with oral antibiotics is that skin tends to improve as long as you swallow the pills. Once you complete the prescription, the acne often returns. And the side effects of eating antibiotics can leave you feeling washed out and with a tendency toward diarrhea, gas, or stomach cramps.

The superdrug for severe acne is oral isotretinoin (marketed as Accutane), a vitamin A derivative that has revolutionized acne therapy. It's the drug of choice for severe cystic acne, the kind that is deep and disfiguring; it's not for the odd pimple here and there. Only your doctor can prescribe this medication, the use of which requires initial CBC (complete blood count), liver function, triglyceride and cholesterol levels before treatment, with reassessment of each test (except CBC) every two weeks.

Side effects include dryness of skin, particularly the lips, palms of the hands, and soles of the feet, as well as the conjunctiv of the eyes. Muscular pains, especially of the back and legs, can also result. Accutane is usually prescribed for five months in the United States; in order to avoid some of the side effects, a lower dosage—but a longer period of treatment—is popular in Europe.

One cardinal rule: Hands Off! "Absolutely no acne lesion should be scratched, picked, or squeezed; that's the worst thing that you can do," warns Victor. This kind of unauthorized messing around can cause deeper infection or scarring. Doctors perform what they call acne surgery—the professional opening and clearing of blackheads, whiteheads, pimples, and cysts and the only kind you should consider. Don't even *think* about buying something called a "blackhead extractor"—it can drive an infection deeper into the skin or spread it over a wider area. The laying on of hands always makes things look worse.

Whether you have mild or severe acne, the key is to *be gentle.* Don't use a washcloth or loofah—they can hold bacteria and reinfect the area. The abrasive pads (Buf-Pufs) are too rough on tender or inflamed skin, and they too can reinfect your face. Use your hands to wash your face, and if it's particularly broken out, dry with disposable paper toweling rather than a cloth towel. Apply any topical medication before you put on moisturizer and sunscreen. When you moisturize, try to avoid any inflamed areas or broken skin.

UN-ACNES AND OTHER WOES

Acne vulgaris, or common acne, is the term for true acne, caused by the complex interrelation between hormones, bacteria, and oil taking place under the skin. But in recent years a new term, *acne cosmetica,* has emerged to describe the breakouts caused by makeup and skin-care products. These eruptions look like common acne, but rather than beginning under the skin, this type of acne starts on the skin surface where products clog pores, trapping oil and skin debris, which leads to pimples. "Clini-

cally, we can't tell any difference between this type of acne and 'true' acne," Victor says. "But if you break out within a week or two after using a new product, that's your clue." A hint: Products containing isopropyl mysitate are comedogenic; that is, they tend to clog pores. The new state-of-the-art hair mousses and shaping gels are also culprits. If you develop small bumps or a cluster of blackheads around your hairline or on your forehead soon after you've begun using a new product, you can be pretty sure what's causing them. Just discontinue use of any suspicious article and try and over-the-counter benzoyl peroxide gel to hasten healing. Read product labels: Try to find items that are oil free (although oil is not the only ingredient that can cause a breakout).

SUN-DRUG INTERACTIONS

Some medications are *photosensitizing,* that is, combined with the sun, they can result in a painful rash after only minutes of sun exposure. (And they're yet another reason to stroke on sunscreen.) The offending medications are some oral antibiotics, diuretics, and tranquilizers. Ask your doctor and your pharmacist to find out if any drugs you're taking are likely to be photosensitizing.

Sunscreen allergies: The chemicals in sunscreen preparations can lead to an allergic reaction in some individuals. As I've said, PABA is the traditional culprit, but relatively few products on the market today contain this ingredient. Still, some men react to other active ingredients, such as cinnamate or benzophenone. Because sunscreen is such a vital part of your skin-care regime, should you find yourself breaking out after applying sunscreen, see a dermatologist, who will do a patch test to determine which product is causing the problem.

Heat rash: This is most common in the summertime, when tight clothes that don't breathe can block sweat ducts, according to Victor. The chest and back are likely sites because that's where men sweat the most. Loose cotton clothing and oil-free sunscreens are the way to go.

THE SWEET SMELL OF NOTHING

I recommend fragrance-free products because it's often the perfumes and fragrances in skin products that cause allergic reaction. That's not to say, however, that unscented lotions won't cause trouble or that a moisturizer with fragrance necessarily will. And to make things even more complicated, some items labeled "unscented" are anything but; they actually contain "masking" fragrances intended to hide the naturally unpleasant odor of some ingredients in the product. Buy a sample or small size of any new product before investing in an industrial-size supply. None of the items I suggest in this book will break your bank, and you can test whether or not something works for you.

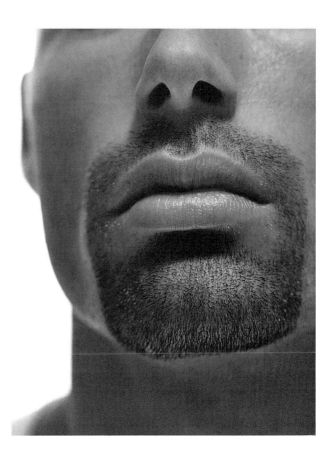

SKIN CANCER

Skin cancers are the most common cancers, and for the most part, while classified as malignancies, doctors don't even think of them as cancers because they are usually curable. They appear most often on the sun-exposed areas of the skin, so you may want to reevaluate that quest for a golden-brown tan that's been eluding you since high school. Doctors now suspect that the mechanism causing skin cancer may be triggered by an earlier sunburn, perhaps going back to childhood. But you're all grown up now, so it's daily applications of sunscreen, avoiding the peak sun hours between 10:00 A.M. and 2:00 P.M., and an annual appointment with your dermatologist for a body check, or a thorough examination of your entire skin, including the scalp, for any suspicious lesions or a mole that changes shape or size. You should examine yourself as well; no one knows your own constellation of freckles, moles, and skin imperfections as well as you do. Most men have moles or freckles they've had since forever—childhood, at least. But since you don't have eyes in the back of your head, enlist a lover or

spouse or friend to inspect those areas you can't see. If you have any suspicions, take them to the doctor—for reassurance if nothing's wrong and early treatment if something is. The good news is that skin cancer is the most treatable of all carcinomas if detected early. So pay attention and see your dermatologist once a year.

BODY HAIR REMOVAL

Body hair is a matter of taste and personal preoccupation. Your culture and genetic inheritance determine how hirsute you are and how happy you are with what you've got.

Hairiness seems to go in and out of fashion. Every four years, when we all catch Olympic fever, the sight of all those sleek swimmers may inspire some furry guys to take it all off. Many athletes shave to reduce aerodynamic drag and to get a certain look. For those of us with more modest athletic aspirations, the razor is one technique. But

shaving has to be done almost every day. Either you get used to the procedure or it gets to be a drag (not the aerodynamic kind). Let's look at some other solutions.

CLIPPING

If shaving every day is uncomfortable for you, leaving stubble and an itchy rash (the unfortunate result of regrowth over sensitive areas), consider clipping as an option. It doesn't pretend to give a smooth, sleek finish; rather, it maintains the hair and looks neat, with a crisp texture and pleasant feel—the difference between an unkempt shag rug and a short-pile plush (for all those of you who don't have an uncle in the carpet business). Clipping avoids the nicks, irritations, and potential for ingrown hairs common to shaving and waxing and takes only a few minutes. Clipping can be done on the chest, back, arms, and legs. Use the old-fashioned electric clippers that barbers use. Oster and Wahl make dependable models with attachments that vary the lengths of the clipped hair. You only need to maintain clipped hair once every couple of weeks, depending on your rate of regrowth and the look you want.

ELECTROLYSIS

This is the only method of hair removal that's considered permanent. It consists of the introduction of a very fine needle into the individual hair follicles. Electric current is then passed through the needle and zaps the bulb of the hair root, thus destroying it. With no root to anchor it, the hair is then removed easily with tweezers and the electrologist moves on to another hair. As you might imagine, this can be a long, tedious process, and it requires patience, a certain tolerance for discomfort, and a considerable investment of time and money. Depending on the amount and the texture of the hair, a session can last anywhere from 10 minutes to a couple of hours. "But for anywhere from a small area of hair, such as a patch on each shoulder or the space between the eyebrows, to the entire back, this method gives good results," notes New York City electrologist Stephanie Donnelly. The skin is cleansed with alcohol and each needle used is disposable. Afterward, the skin is calmed with a soothing lotion—and that's it.

WAXING

Electrolysis is the only really permanent solution for unwanted hair, but its expense and the time involved rule it out for some men. For a larger job, such as a truly furry back, "electrolysis isn't always feasible," notes Mary Ann De Luccy, an electrologist and aesthetician practicing in New York City. Her recommen-

dation to men who seek longer-lasting smoothness is waxing. This involves the application of warm-to-hot wax over the skin. Then a strip of fabric is pressed into the wax and quickly and deftly stripped off—voila!—and the skin is left satiny and hair free. But don't try this at home. Although you can buy home-waxing kits, the procedure can be unbelievably messy—something like pulling a not-very-tasty taffy all over the room you're in. And it takes an experienced operator to whisk off hair and not the skin. But the results can last between four and six weeks. Some men develop a red rash, the result of the physical pull of the fabric strip, as well as an allergic reaction to the chemicals in the wax, but this irritation subsides in a matter of hours.

LASERS

Recently there's been a lot of ballyhoo about laser hair removal, a technique performed in tony day spas and costing well over a thousand dollars. It's all very high tech: The area to be treated is coated with a graphite powder, and then the technician uses a laser light over the area. Since the laser can distinguish be-

tween colors, it is supposed to "read" only the graphite-covered body part and remove the hair there. De Luccy explains the drawbacks: "The graphite powder doesn't always adhere perfectly to each hair shaft—where it doesn't, the laser won't do what it should." But the idea is intriguing and appealing for those men who are unhappy with their hair, and the technology may catch up in a few years. Meanwhile, other options can be explored with a high degree of success and satisfaction.

ATHLETE'S FOOT AND NAIL FUNGUS: SOLE SEARCHING

The athlete's foot of locker-room nightmares is actually a more complex condition than you might think. Caused either by dermatophytes (fungi that feast on dead tissues like nails and the outer layers of the skin) or yeast, infections can begin between the toes, on the soles of the feet, or on the toenails. In an acute infection, you can get blisters that itch like crazy or cracking between the toes that's both itchy and

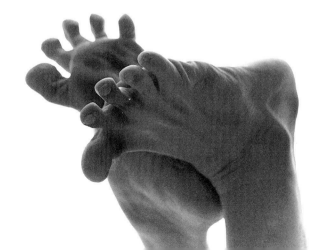

painful. In a chronic infection of *T. rubrum,* you might have a "moccasin" pattern of red, scaly thickening skin on the soles of your feet. Help!

If you're in generally good health, you could start with an over-the-counter product like Tinactin or Lotrimin. Meanwhile, good hygiene is essential and can prevent subsequent outbreaks: Dry carefully between the toes after bathing. Dust powder between toes and inside your shoes to absorb moisture. Change footwear daily, untying laces and flipping out the tongue and airing the shoes for 24 hours. Once your skin has calmed down, these preventive measures should keep the problem at bay.

But if this routine doesn't help after a few days, see a doctor. Athlete's foot may be complicated by a secondary bacterial infection, and what looks like athlete's foot may in fact be eczema, psoriasis, or dermatitis, an allergic reaction to the materials in your shoes, especially adhesives and dyes. The *T. rubrum* ("moccasin") fungus usually will not respond to topical preparations, but requires short-term use of an oral antifungal medication. And if you have diabetes or circulatory problems or are taking medication for other conditions, treatment may be more complex. Dr. Glenn B. Weiss, a podiatrist practicing in New York City, notes, "Every foot fungus infection has its own distinguishing characteristic and needs to be evaluated in order for the patient to get the best treatment."

This is particularly important if you have nail fungus, an ugly and often embarrassing condition in which the nails become thick and flaky, sometimes separating from the toe. There are many reasons men develop thickened toenails: fungus, psoriasis, diabetes, circulatory changes, and plain old wear and tear. Chronic problems won't be solved with over-the-counter products, but new oral medications available by prescription seem to be most effective. Follow all the directions as you would with any other medication.

Results may not be visible for months due to the slow pace at which toenails grow. It takes six months from start to finish for a nail to grow out. Your nails may not look as they once did, but the improvement will be dramatic. There are many treatments available today.

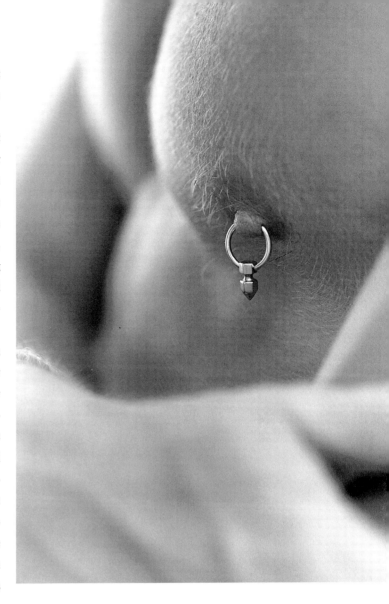

TATTOOING AND PIERCING

Sailors, merchant marines, bikers, servicemen, and cops were the types that would proudly display a tattoo on their chest or arm. But today tattoos are everywhere! The most unlikely places, such as ankles and biceps, not to mention buttocks and foreheads, are where tattoos are showing up, but who is sporting tattoos is the real news here. Men and women of all ages, backgrounds, and social status are proudly displaying artful and imaginative designs from around the world.

Out of the dark back rooms where tattoo artists once hid, to the store fronts and upscale tattoo specialty shops, the body as an art gallery is defining the next millennium. Our pop icons are not the only bearers of this once seemingly decadent rite, but now super models, travel

agents, bank tellers, and even a grade school cook (my sister) have tattoos.

If you are considering a tattoo or a piercing, you should investigate and shop around—ask to see pictures of finished work. If you think about what the artist is about to do to your dermis, you might want to know whom you are dealing with. States are now legalizing and licensing tattoo parlors and the artists that paint in your skin. Blood is the issue. Tattoos are drawn on a permanent layer of skin, down past the semipermanent epidermis. If sterile procedure is followed, the blood risk is minimal. Therefore, your risk depends on the professionalism of the artist you have chosen.

Pain is another component of tattooing that depends on where you have the tattoo placed. The more fat in the area you choose, the less pain you will have. The wrists, ankles, the inside of the upper arm, and the back of the neck are areas where there is little fat and more sensitivity. Pain is part of the tattoo; trying to avoid this essential component by drinking alcohol prior to the session is not advisable. Aside from impairing your judgment as to what designs look good at the time, the alcohol will thin your blood and make you bleed more. And just as the pain of exercising helps you to appreciate the gains in your health, so too the feeling of the tattoo process enhances your appreciation of the art. The sensation has been described to me in several ways, from a mosquito bite to a slight scratch repeated over and over. A young man told me that he had to dissociate himself from the process and detach his arm from his body mentally. In his experience, the pain of the actual tattooing process is small compared to the itching that accompanied the healing process. Well, anything for art! Just make sure you have a qualified artist who is sanitary, reputable, and makes you feel comfortable.

Tattoo removal is now becoming more possible due to advances in technology with lasers. Dermatologists are performing this treatment in their offices as a pain-free alternative to other methods of tattoo removal, but the cost of the treatment is still extreme. Choose your design well!

The phenomenon of body ornamentation has made its way into our popular culture recently. It may seem extreme to put a steel rod through your nipple or a ring through your nose, but to many it is a self-expression or an ornament they desire. From the tasteful to the outrageous, piercing ears is conservative compared to the other body parts, such as eyelids, the navel, the tongue, the penis, and the scrotum, all now donning rings, studs, and posts.

Consider where you put this new ornament and make sure you realize the healing process may take longer than you think. The navel can take months due to the lack of blood flow to the area and can be quite painful. The tongue is also quite popular, but can easily become infected. Hygiene and cleanliness are vital to prevent a painful infection from occurring, which could lead to more dangerous side effects.

This is a big decision and to make it hastily or on a whim might be more than you bargained for. Consider the consequences and then do what you feel. You can also just let the hole grow back in if you choose. Just remove the post or ring and the skin will take care of itself.

SPAS

Men are becoming more aware of the taboo world of the spa. Spas were once considered a domain for the rich and famous, a well-kept secret that only a few had the privilege to enjoy. Those days are over and the "pamper me" mentality has finally made its way into the men's world. In many health clubs these days you will find hot tubs, saunas, and steam rooms as amentities that are built onto the locker room and massage therapy as an added service to the other à la carte services offered.

The spa has come into its own. Day spas are open all over the United States and other countries to offer services to men and women who want to find peace, to relax, and to reduce stress by being pampered and looked after like royalty.

In these day spas you will find an array of services that range from herbal wraps and mud baths to electrolysis and massage. Men are having pedicures, manicures,

and facials on a regular basis. These services were once thought a strictly women's desire, but the doors have been pushed open by men who want the same attention and skilled services to help give them a groomed and well-kept appearance.

The day spas in the urban areas are by appointment only, but then there are the spas that are situated in some of the most beautiful parts of our country and the world. From the beaches of St. Barts in the Caribbean to the north of France, the deserts of Arizona, and the hills of Wisconsin, you can find a spa that will exfoliate your skin, soak you in hot springs, open your senses with aroma therapy, and clean out your colon. The list of services is endless, so call and have brochures sent to you, or drop in and ask for information at the front desk. Services like Spa Finders or a travel agent can help suggest a spa in your price range and guide you to the right spa for your specific requirements.

Spas specialize in creating a calming and tranquil atmosphere; they are built that way, carefully laid out so that you can relax and let go of the stress induced by your job or other obstacles that affect you. These spas can also be expensive, not only peeling a layer of stress off your brain but a chunk of cash out of your checkbook.

If cost is the only deterrent for you, then you can also consider buying some products that you can apply yourself to get that pampered feeling. Many amenities are now being offered over the counter in specialty stores and even at your hair salon. Candles, soaps and salts, oils and ointments can be purchased at any price, depending on the brand name, and applied or administered in the privacy of your own home. Take the opportunity to relax and enjoy just existing. Smell the roses!

CHAPTER TEN

Diet Basics

HOW TO EAT REALISTICALLY

How to eat and eating are very different realities when it comes to eating healthy. Men seem to have a more difficult time watching what they eat instead of how much they eat. A simple and easy way around this problem could be to imagine yourself sitting at the table in front of a plate. A paper plate that you would use at an outing or cookout. The type that has portion compartments molded into the plate.

Normal Americans would load up the largest compartment with the burger, the steak, the ribs, or the ham, leaving the smaller compartments for fruits, vegetables, and grain foods (things you don't find at a cookout).

Turn the plate around. Switch the compartments around in order to have the vegetables in the largest compartments and the meat in one of the smaller ones. This will decrease your fat intake without your feeling deprived or cheated. You can still enjoy the ham and steak and all those things that taste so good, but in a quantity that will promote weight loss and help you to reorganize the way you eat. When you finish the plate, you are done and have eaten as much as you should. If you are still hungry, eat more of the grains or veggies. Or pass on seconds and eat fruit for dessert.

Reevaluate and reorganize how much you eat and what you eat. These are the two key issues that most people have to consider when attempting a weight-management program.

SHOP 'TIL YOU DROP

Shopping for food has to be examined. It seems as though stores are set up to sell us whatever is at eye level: the tastiest food, packaged in the most attractive boxes, bags, and cans. This is all done suggestively by the grocer and the people who bring you these taste treats, which we have all enjoyed but which may have caused you to suffer the consequences of gaining fat. While you are at the store, try filling up your cart in reverse, putting the fruits and vegetables in the large part and filling the fold-down child's seat with the meats and fatty items. This simple yet effective way of reorganizing your nutritional intake will only guide you down the right path of success.

FAST FOOD DOESN'T MEAN FAT FOOD

Just because you rely on the Golden Arches and the King to feed you doesn't mean you have to become supersized and shake your way into a 38-waist trouser. These chains can offer you nutrition and easy access to food, as we humans need to eat, without having to compromise the newly found interest in cutting fat from your diet.

If you choose to go the fast-food route, try eating anything that comes grilled. Choose a salad with Italian dressing over the creamy dressings, and take super sizing literally. Some fast chains offer baked potatoes, but you have to determine what goes on the spud. Eat it plain instead of drowning it with cheese and sour cream. You are going down the right path, but you are getting sidetracked by your taste buds.

Also, remember that "all you can eat" doesn't mean "TODAY"! Sometimes a single serving is not enough, so go back for more, but use your judgment.

FEEDING THE FIRE

If you were burning a fire in a fireplace, you would build that fire with kindling wood and bunched-up paper. A match would ignite the flames and the fire would burn brightly with a roar. As the flames began to burn with less intensity, you would throw on a log or two to keep the fire burning; then the fire would burn slower and with a steady flickering of the flames.

You may ask, "What does this have to do with anything?" Well, if you think of your body's metabolism as a fire (metabolism being the number of calories you burn at any given moment), the fire that burns fat stored on your body, you will begin to see the correlation. Imagine the fat-burning process as a fire in the fireplace. What you throw into the fire represents how the flame will burn. If you throw in kindling wood, the flames burn with great intensity and quickly burn out. If you throw a log on the fire, the flame burns slowly and lasts much longer.

Now try to think of kindling wood as a small meal, one that would trigger your metabolism to react by burning fat and help with the digestive process. Your body will break down the food into energy (glucose) and store supplied energy for later use. That is what that love handle is or the layer of fat in front of your six-pack of abs. Depending on the size of the meal, your metabolism will work until it is satisfied. When the amount of food your body requires has been digested and metabolized your body will go for stored fat until it is finished and then rests.

The log represents a large meal, steak, mashed potatoes, vegetables, bread and butter, dessert, and a beverage. That is a big log! Throw that on the fire and it would smolder for hours. Our metabolism would attack the meal as it would with the kindling, but then would die down after a while, because the system doesn't work that long. The only exercise here is eating that delicious meal, although the consequences are simple—nutrition, of course, but you are storing fat and wasting food at the same time. The by-products of that tasty meal get pushed through your system as waste and the rest as stored fat.

About 3,500 calories in reserve (stored fat) equals one pound of fat on your body. Let that log burn down until you need to trigger the flames again. Then the metabolism will look for energy to burn on its own until it is satisfied. That is why the effect of eating smaller meals will help you boost the metabolic reaction and keep it working until it has taken what it needs. If it needs more than it is given (like all of us, but that's another chapter), it will go to the storage unit, and that means loss of stored fat—weight loss.

EATING TO GROW AND EATING TO SHRINK

The more effective way to eat for weight management, in either direction—plus or minus, is to eat five times a day. Five small meals, or three moderate-sized meals and two snacks, seem to work for most everyone. It all depends on what you are eating and what you are trying to achieve as your goal.

For weight loss, I would recommend a maximum of 2,000 calories a day with a side order of 30 to 45 minutes of aerobic exercise. I know the media reports about 20 minutes a day of moderate exercise will help you to lose weight, but most people would like to lose weight by tonight. Researchers also provided the media with the information that the same 20 minutes they targeted before could be accumulated over the entire day. I encourage everyone to get up off their behinds and exercise and eat right, but trusting your entire weight-loss success to 20 minutes of *accumulated* aerobic activity and a low-fat diet may prove unrealistic and unsuccessful.

CHAPTER ELEVEN

Soul Training

THE MIND/BODY CONNECTION

MENTAL FITNESS

"We meditate, not to tune out, but to tune in; not to get away from it all, but to get in touch with it all." —Deepak Chopra

In a typical day we think approximately 60,000 thoughts. If you think that is astounding, 90 percent of those thoughts are repeated from the day before, and then repeated from the days and weeks before that. Psychology tells us that thought patterns are developed at very early ages, and then repeat themselves over and over throughout our lives.

Thought patterns and simple thoughts believed to fall into the realm of mental health play an important role in overall wellness and physical health. Science has proven without a doubt that the nervous system, the immune system, and the endocrine system "talk" to one another constantly.

MEDITATION AND FITNESS

Your thoughts and emotions are constantly affecting the trillions of cells in your body. When you are relaxed and calm, chemical messengers such as endorphins and serotonin are released from the brain into the rest of the system, creating a sense of well-being and harmony. In a state of mental or emotional stress, however, the response is to guard or defend the system. This in itself is not neg-

ative. However, repeated activation of the stress response exhausts the adrenal glands, lowers the immune function, and can cause stress-related disease.

Meditation seeks to introduce a new level of "fitness" as to how you think, feel, and perceive the world around you. With the stress and anxieties created by today's lifestyle, we could all benefit greatly by incorporating a simple meditation practice into our daily routine.

Scientific studies conclude that simple meditation practices of 20 to 30 minutes result in a decrease of the body's oxygen consumption—almost twice the decrease produced during sleep. Studies also show lower blood pressure levels decrease the amount of excess stomach acids and reduce the secretion of stress hormones. Psychological problems such as anxiety, depression, and hostility are greatly reduced through meditation. The practice can help you see life as a challenge rather than an obstacle.

WHAT IS MEDITATION?

The truth is that meditation has been practiced in many cultures throughout the ages and is not necessarily a religious activity. With practice, you can learn to move into a deeper place of relaxation. The goal is to achieve "pure awareness," or consciousness. To define pure awareness is impossible. Scientists, spiritual leaders, philosophers, and psychologists have spent lifetimes trying to define this apparently simple yet timeless subject. The term most frequently used to describe our "being" is *spirit*. Spirit is defined as the animating force of life. Many great teachers throughout the ages have said that spirit can be found in the space *between* our thoughts. To find this place we must slow down and look inward.

LOOKING INWARD

The challenge of looking inward or moving into pure awareness is to let go of any attachment to our thoughts. Our mind seems to conduct a one-way conversation with itself. Most often our thoughts are focused on the past or the future.

We rarely live in the richness and fullness of the present moment. The present moment is what is real, and living in it is the goal most of us want to achieve.

PRACTICING MEDITATION

There are many variations of meditation techniques: those taught in specific Yoga practices; those taught by fellowships or by spiritual leaders, health-care groups, stress-reduction groups; and those that are self-taught. Three practices more commonly used in the Western minds include:

*Watching the breath

*Object concentration

*Reciting a mantra

• **Watching the Breath.** Observe your breath while sitting quietly. Thoughts will move through your mind, but your attention stays on your breath. Follow your breath as it flows in and out of your lungs. Notice the space between the "in and out" breaths. If your mind wanders—and it most likely will—simply bring it back to the breath. Watching the breath helps you achieve the realization that you are not your thoughts but something that goes beyond your thoughts.

• **Object Concentration.** Focus your gaze on a single object. An inspirational object is most helpful, like a flower or stream. Many gaze

lightly into the flame of a candle. The goal is to bring the mind to one point of focus in the present moment.

- **Mantra Meditation.** Mantra means "control of mind." In mantra meditation you repeat a word or series of words to help you gain control of a restless mind. The mantra doesn't have to be of foreign origin. Simple yet powerful words—"joy, peace, bliss" or "peace, harmony, and well-being"—are very effective.

To realize the benefits of meditation, a regular practice is required. Just as you train your body through a consistent program of exercise, in meditation you train your mind through consistent practice. You open up to new levels of mental clarity, physical health, and spiritual inspiration.

Practical exercise: Get a tape recorder and set it down if front of you. Put on a New Age CD or open the window and let the environmental sounds be the music. Read the following text into the recorder as if you were telling a bedtime story to a child or a good friend you haven't seen in many years. Take your time and read it through once before you put it on tape and record it. If you feel embarrassed you could have your someone special do it, or a parent. You can use this as a way of destressing yourself and exercising your imagination. Use the (. . .) as pauses.

THE DIALOGUE

Let's begin by taking a comfortable position. Breathe in and out slowly and fully, feeling the blood flow through the body and your body resting in place. Relax and feel the force of gravity blanket your body lightly . . . take a couple of deep, cleansing breaths. Focus your attention on each part of your body, invite your body to release and relax any tension that may be stored or isolated in one spot, and then merely allow it to release in its own way. . . .

Focus your awareness on your feet and invite your feet to

release and relax any tension they may be holding . . . notice the beginning sensations of relaxation in your feet . . . invite the muscles of the your calves and shins to release. . . . notice and allow your lower legs to relax in their own way, becoming more comfortable and at ease. . . . Remember, as each part of your body relaxes, all of your body relaxes more easily. . . .

Invite your thighs and hamstrings to release and relax . . . allow your hips and pelvis to join in this letting go of stress and tension . . . your lower back and buttocks join in releasing and relaxing any tension that may be there. . . .

Invite your abdomen to relax . . . the muscles of your abdomen and your midback . . . to join in this deeper, more comfortable state of relaxation . . . invite the organs in your abdominal cavity to also join in this letting go, this release . . . and just allow that whole lower half of your body to let go and become even more deeply comfortable and at ease . . . invite your chest muscles and the muscles between your shoulder blades to release and relax . . . becoming soft and at ease . . . the organs in your chest joining in this deeper, more comfortable state. . . .

Imagine your shoulders and neck muscles becoming soft, releasing any tension that might be there . . . allowing them to take a well-deserved rest . . . and this relaxation flowing down over your shoulders into your upper arms . . . elbows . . . forearms . . . wrists . . . and hands. . . .

Invite all the small muscles of your hands . . . in between the fingers . . . to release and relax and become very comfortable . . . your index fingers . . . middle fingers . . . ring fingers . . . little fingers . . . and your thumbs . . . deeply relaxed . . . all the way to the very tips. . . .

Allow your scalp and forehead to release and relax any tension that may be there . . . becoming soft and smooth. . . . the muscles of your face soft and at ease . . . allowing a very pleasant sense of relaxation to come into the small muscles around your eyes . . . letting go of the tension throughout your face and jaw . . . neck and shoulders . . . all the way down . . . as your body relaxes more deeply, your mind becomes quiet and peaceful as well. . . .

Now to deepen this comfortable state of relaxation and concentration, imagine yourself at the top of a stairway that has 10 steps leading down from where you stand . . . let it be any kind of stairway . . . one you have seen before or one that you just make up . . . notice how steep they are or how wide the steps might be. . . .

When you are ready, begin to descend the staircase one step at a time, counting backward from 10 to 1 as you go . . . allowing yourself to feel more deeply, more comfortably relaxed with each step you descend . . . let this imaginary staircase help you reach an even deeper level of mind and body with each step down . . . 10 . . . 9 . . . deeper and more relaxed . . . 8 . . . 7 . . . softly and slowly . . . 6 . . . each step takes you deeper . . . 5 . . . halfway down . . . 4 . . . nothing to worry about . . . 3 . . . 2 . . . and 1 . . . at the bottom of the stairs . . . very comfortable and relaxed in body and mind. . . .

To further deepen your relaxation, imagine yourself now in a very beautiful, peaceful place. . . . This might be somewhere you have visited before or somewhere you might make up in your imagination . . . just let the image of the place come to you . . . like a picture coming into focus. . . . It really doesn't matter what kind of place you imagine as long as it's beautiful,

quiet, and serene. . . . Let this be a special inner place for you . . . somewhere that you feel particularly at ease . . . where you feel secure . . . a place to be quiet and reflective . . . somewhere healing for you. . . . It could be a real place like a meadow or a beach . . . or an imaginary place like floating in the air. . . .

Let yourself explore this quiet, imaginary place . . . notice what you see there . . . what sounds you hear . . . even the smells that you sense there . . . notice especially what it feels like to be there, and immerse yourself in the beauty, the feelings of peacefulness. . . .

Take some time to relax into the deep feelings of peacefulness, quiet, and healing you can sense in this spot . . . take as much time as you need. . . . (long pause).

When you are ready, prepare yourself to come back to your waking state. Remember, this is your special inner place, a place you can return to at any time . . . a place within you where healing and peace are always available . . . a place that is always with you. . . .

To return to waking, but bringing back with you the sense of peacefulness you have experienced here, all you need to do is to recall the imaginary staircase that brought you here . . . imagine yourself at the bottom of the stairs . . . with 10 steps up . . . as you ascend the stairs, you become more and more awake and alert . . . aware of your surroundings. . . . When you reach the top of the stairs, let yourself come awake, refreshed . . . feeling better than you did before. . . .

One . . . 2 . . . coming up, becoming more awake . . . 3 . . . 4 . . . bringing back with you a sense of peace and relaxation . . . 5 . . . 6 . . . feeling refreshed and rested, like you have had a good nap . . . 7 . . . 8 . . . becoming more alert and awake with each step . . . your eyes may begin to open . . . 9 . . . and 10 . . . at the top of the stairs and wide awake . . . smile . . . stretch . . . alert and refreshed.

Use this tape as you would use aspirin. Sometimes it will be all you need to get hold of some feelings you want to understand, or to get the rest that your body needs. It's a simple way to connect with your physical side, which so many of us run, jog, push, and pull away from everyday. Introduce yourself to you and your feelings, both physical and emotional. You may even like the person you find.

Many men will have a difficult time experiencing deep relaxation due to the fact that they may feel emotional or sad and this may be uncomfortable. It is natural to feel sad, and no one ever died from feelings as the cause, so look at your feelings as you would a new aspect of your workout routine and then move on. Your body stores feelings and memories in the muscles, and when you relax and let your mind and body relax, emotions and feelings will surface. Let them bubble up and come out; you will feel better and you will also have learned something about yourself.

Repeat the following stretch a few times before you start your meditation or relaxation period. It will promote the oxygen and blood flow through the body and help you connect to your thoughts better. Go slowly and repeat the stretch about 10 times. After you finish just sit or lie on the floor and enjoy.

YOGA LUNGE

Taken right out of the yoga centers for your benefit, this posture concentrates on balance as well as breath. Start out standing with your arms at your side and your abdominals held firm. Take a giant step backward with one foot and adjust to maintain your balance. Try to keep the leg behind you extended as long as possible, with as little a bend in the knee as is comfortable. Keep your chest and shoulders up tall in order for the stretch to work. The proper position and attention to technique is vital to feel the benefits of this stretch. This exercise is illustrated on pages 202–203.

Slowly raise your arms in front of you and reach upward over your head. Keep your shoulders down away from your ears, but feel the length of the muscles in the back, the midsection, and the back of the arms. Hold that position and concentrate on the area in front of the pelvis on the same side as the leg behind you. This is your hip flexor, one of the most overused and abused muscles in the body. It requires more flexibility training than other muscles.

Give yourself the opportunity to focus on your breath and balance during this stretch. This stretch is very sculptural and statuesque, as well as necessary and beneficial. Bring your arms back down in front of your body and then to your sides, and return to a standing position. Repeat the stretch, changing the leg position only. The arms perform the same movement as they did before. Balance and breath, focus and form, the perfect prescription for almost everything.

EPILOGUE

Looking at these remarkable images and reading these words should give you a better understanding of what steps it takes to get fit and live a healthier life. It's up to you now. Be patient, be consistent, be committed.

GOOD LUCK!

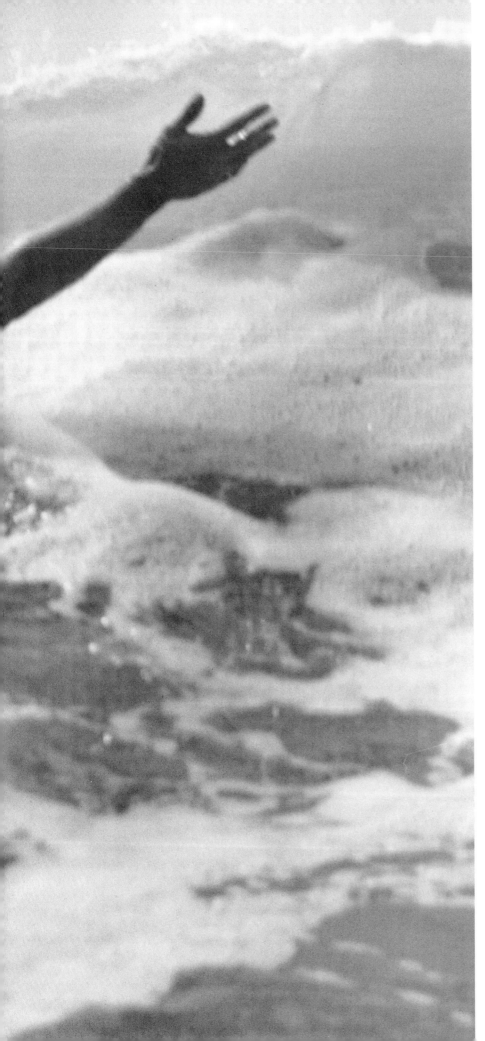

Index

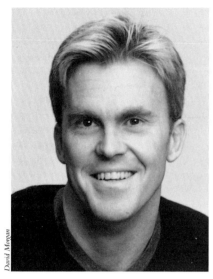

David Morgan

ABOUT THE AUTHOR

JON GISWOLD is a certified group exercise instructor and personal trainer who teaches in New York's most prominent fitness centers, including the Reebok Sports Club/NY. Jon has starred in his own video, choreographed twelve exercise videos, and has appeared on a variety of television shows. As a leader and volunteer, Jon is a member of the National Leadership Council of the Workout for Hope, which benefits the AIDS/HIV research department of the City of Hope. Born and raised in Grantsburg, Wisconsin, Jon now lives in New York City.

ABOUT THE PHOTOGRAPHER

DAVID MORGAN began shooting professionally in 1975 during a successful theater career and quickly established himself as one of New York's most innovative headshot photographers. In 1989, in the Fire Island Pines, he provided a provocative poster image for the musical *Anything Goes*, his first male nude image, and his photography career took a sudden and unexpected turn. The following year he created his signature work, *The White Party,* for the legendary New York City winter dance event. In 1992, designer Greg Sovell chose the photographer to create the stunning black-and-white photographs that launched his highly successful 2(x)ist Underwear line. Morgan has since photographed over fifteen different fashion lines, and a commercial career emerged with magazine work, advertising, and book and CD covers. In 1997, Morgan entered the Worldwide Web with his highly praised commercial site, www.dmny.com. His fine-art photography celebrating the male figure is available worldwide through prints, posters, greeting cards, and postcards.

Ken Miller

ABOUT THE PROJECT DIRECTOR

KEN ROBERTS has had varied careers in his lifetime, from social work to fashion modeling. Currently a literary agent and book packager, he specializes in fine-art photography books and represents authors and photographers worldwide. He resides in New York City.

© David Morgan